HOW TO

HOW TO dj

THE INSIDER'S GUIDE TO SUCCESS ON THE DECKS

**TOM FREDERIKSE
AND PHIL BENEDICTUS**

Point-Blank   PIATKUS

IN ASSOCIATION WITH POINT BLANK

❀ *Visit the Piatkus website!*

Piatkus publishes a wide range of bestselling fiction and non-fiction, including books on health, mind, body & spirit, sex, self-help, cookery, biography and the paranormal.

If you want to:
- read descriptions of our popular titles
- buy our books over the internet
- take advantage of our special offers
- enter our monthly competition
- learn more about your favourite Piatkus authors

VISIT OUR WEBSITE AT: www.piatkus.co.uk

Copyright © 2002 by Point-Blank

First published in Great Britain in 2002 by
Judy Piatkus (Publishers) Limited
5 Windmill Street
London W1T 2JA
e-mail: info@piatkus.co.uk

The moral right of the author has been asserted

A catalogue record for this book is available from the British Library

ISBN 0 7499 2325 3

Edited by Louise Crathorne

Cover, design and setting by The Whole Hog Design Co Ltd

This book has been printed on paper manufactured with respect
for the environment using wood from managed sustainable resources

Printed and bound in Great Britain by Butler & Tanner, Frome, Somerset

HOW TO DJ
THE INSIDER'S GUIDE TO SUCCESS ON THE DECKS

CONTENTS

PART TWO
THE DJ BUSINESS

08 RISING TO THE TOP: WAVE WHEN YOU GET THERE"

PART THREE
THE MUSIC BUSINESS

X

Credit where credit is due:

A huge shout to Rob Cowan for being the best geezer in the business. Cheers to Alice Davis for all your hard work and for believing in us. Thanks to those that made the early years so much fun for me: Sasha, Tommy D, Matthew Roberts, Frankie Foncett and Allister Whitehead. But most of all, thank you Mishy, for everything. Love and Respeck – Tom.

Big up yerself: Rob Cowan – you made it all happen, Tanya Benedictus for making me happen, the brothers, Luke and Dan 'The Incredible' Benedictus – props, boo, respect. And to all the great friends who have partied with me over the years; big love to one and all; keep it real, a'right? Special thanks are also due to DMC in Sydney for provision of the finest mixing equipment in the Asia Pacific region at ridiculously short notice and to the boys at Cola Records for their brilliance and dedication – Phil.

Suzy 'The Boss' Crowley, Risto at Arbiter Group, Damon and Jojo at Numark Alesis, Graham and Fiona at Lewisham Council, Andy and Mark at the Karrot Project, Martin and Claire at GLLaB, Helen at Include, Everyone at DJ Magazine, Moose at the Ministry of Sound, Keeney-Mancini, Andy at Avision, Chris Elwell-Sutton, Niall Hampton, Allan at Red Sound, Mike Benson, Peter at Jack Ross, Graham 'Hound' Massey, All Point-Blank students past and present, Janet and Karlene at the Crib, Wilma at Shoreditch New Deal Trust, Stuart Cameron at Newham, Sam Mann at the Mirror, Jeanette Cunningham at Greenwich, Amelia Pinsent at Hot Tickets, David Gordois at News of the World, Sandie Tozer at Time Out, Rob at the Medicine Bar, James at the Pool Bar – Rob and Point-Blank.

PART ONE

GEAR & TECHNIQUE

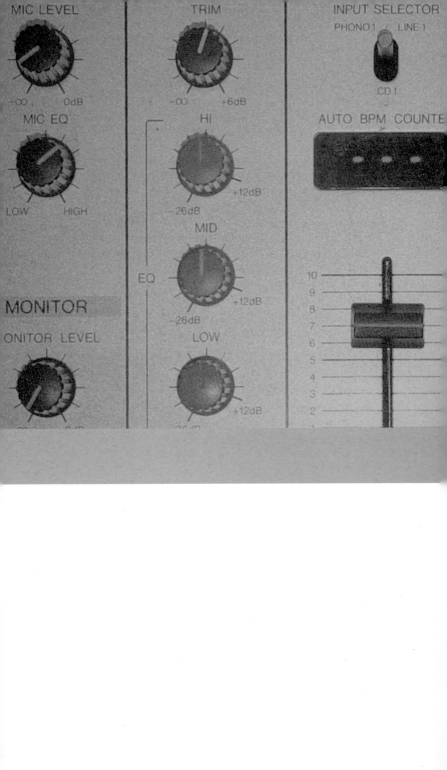

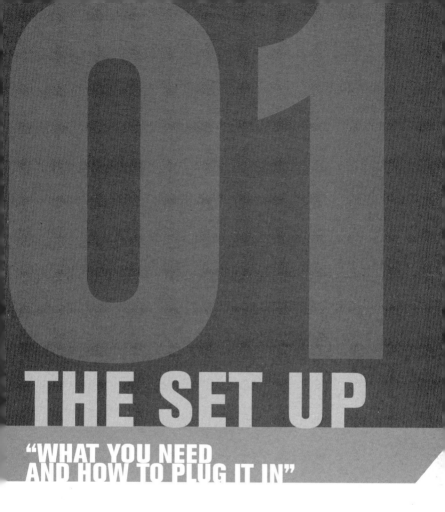

01

THE SET UP

"WHAT YOU NEED AND HOW TO PLUG IT IN"

As long as you know what kit you need and how to work it, you don't really need to understand it. You just have to be able to get the equipment to play your tunes, which, fortunately, is what it is designed to do. Frankly, the most complicated tool a DJ uses is his or her own body.

And we're talking about familiar components here, like turntables, which still play records. It's just that the ones DJs use have a few extra features. OK, so a 'disco mixer' is not standard issue with most HiFi systems, but it is basically just a glorified stereo, which happens to be dedicated to mixing different sounds. The sound systems in clubs are bigger, more powerful versions of what you have at home, and while there may be a bit more complicated equipment you, as a DJ, are probably not even allowed to breathe on it; it's somebody else's problem.

So this is the first thing to remember: the machines are on your side. They will do what you tell them.

>> THE SOUND SYSTEM

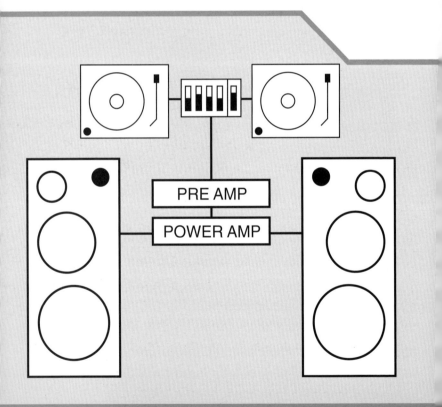

Figure 1: A classic club sound system demonstrating how the components work together

‖ Players

First up, are the bits that actually play the records: turntables, CD players, MP3 players, Minidisc players, DAT players, and whatever else a clubowner might think of. These are the units that actually produce the music (the 'signal') that will eventually be amplified over the system.

‖ Mixers

The disco mixer serves two purposes: to boost the signal as a 'pre-amplifier' and to allow the DJ to blend different music sources. This louder signal is then passed on through to the amplifiers.

‖ Amplifiers

These boost the sound. Amps can be any size, from as small as a briefcase to as large as a desk. Some processing (adjusting the quality of the sound) will take place at this stage whether you can see it or not. Occasionally, amplifiers have 'crossovers' inside them. A crossover separates the sound into high treble and low bass. Often you will see another small box sitting on top of the amp, usually the crossover. You might also see an overall 'EQ' (or equalizer) box sitting on the amp. This also processes the sound to make up for any acoustic problems in the room, and to help the amp seem even better than it is. The amplifier then sends the sound on its way to the speakers.

‖ Speakers

These let the sound loose onto the dancefloor. The sound

may also be sent from the mixer to a second amplifier and from there to a booth monitor speaker (see Chapter 4).

>> TOOLS OF THE TRADE

This is a brief guide to the kind of gear you can expect to encounter as a working DJ: how to set it up and how to use it. This book can tell you almost everything you need to know, but every piece of kit has its own peculiarities so you still need to read the instruction manuals provided.

Turntables

A DJ turntable is similar to a standard home HiFi turntable, but is adapted for club use. There are some specific changes that have been made to make things easier for DJs, but essentially it still plays records, by reading the groove with a tiny diamond (the 'needle') and turning the vibration into an electrical signal.

So what's the difference between a standard turntable and a DJ turntable? For a start, you need to have a very different needle (or 'cartridge') because the stability (or 'tracking') needs to be much better – the needle must stick to the groove at all times. Domestic HiFi systems are all about the best possible sound and the kind of cartridge that delivers the best sound is very delicate, performing best with low weighting on the arm. It wouldn't last two seconds in a club. So for DJ turntables, you need a needle that is tough enough to survive scratch DJs, won't jump when faced with a floor full of pogoing nutters, but still delivers sound faithfully.

This is the first major difference: the DJ cartridge and tone-arm are designed as much with practicality as high fidelity in mind and to this end there has been a recent trend amongst manufacturers to go with a straight tone-arm, to further aid tracking.

Then there's the whole issue of the speed of the records (tempo). A HiFi turntable is designed to play at precisely 33 or 45 rpm, but a DJ turntable has a 'varispeed' (pitch) controller allowing the DJ to slow down or speed up the tune very precisely. The classic DJ turntables, the Technics SL 1200 and 1210, allow you to speed up or slow down the record by up to eight per cent, while newer models might go up to 30% either way. Whatever the percentage, it's there to help the DJ beat mix, passing seamlessly from one record to the next. If you are buying a DJ turntable, make sure that the varispeed controller is quick and precise.

The motor on a DJ turntable should also be strong. It must be able to withstand heavy use at the hands of DJs. It should be unruffled by heavy vibrations. And the motor has to start up and play the record at the right speed at the touch of a button.

Pick up any DJ turntable and you'll see that it's a pretty hefty piece of gear. If you think about clubs, the people who go there and what they get up to, this feature shouldn't be a surprise. One aspect that does vary from one DJ deck to the next is the weight of the disc that the records rest on (the 'platter') which does affect the DJ. You need a lighter touch with a lighter platter, logically enough.

‖ Cartridges

You can spend a small fortune on cartridges and the more pricey ones do, on the whole, perform a bit better. If you have the decks set up right, however, unless you are planning to go scratch crazy, you won't really notice a vast difference. The expensive ones might last a bit longer and skip a bit less, but just because a cartridge looks flash it doesn't mean it's going to sound any better.

‖ Slipmats

The most underrated DJ tool of the lot: the meek, yet mighty, slipmat.

Figure 2: SL1200 with a slip-m

A slipmat is really just a piece of felt that is placed on the platter underneath the record. It allows you to use your finger to stop or spin the record on top of the slipmat. You cannot DJ without slipmats. Without them it is practically impossible to control the record hands-on with any degree of accuracy. So get some decent ones; that means ones that slip a lot.

TIPS

IF YOU FIND YOUR SLIPMAT WON'T SLIP SATISFACTORILY, THEN CHECK THAT THE HOLE IN THE MIDDLE ISN'T TOO TIGHT AROUND THE CENTRE (THE 'SPINDLE').
IF IT IS, JUST SLIGHTLY ENLARGE THE HOLE WITH A KNIFE OR SCISSORS.
IF THIS STILL DOESN'T WORK YOU COULD ALWAYS PUT A BIT OF PLASTIC RECORD SLEEVE UNDERNEATH IF YOU'RE FEELING STINGY. THIS TRICK ALSO ENSURES THE SLIPMATS KEEP WORKING EVEN WHEN THERE IS MOISTURE IN THE AIR IN A SWEATY CLUB.

‖ DJ CD Players and Other Digital Formats

CD players have become increasingly widespread in clubs over the last few years, as they have become more advanced. The modern DJ CD player allows you to cue up to any point in the track, use varispeed and do almost anything you can do with a turntable – models are now available with a 'virtual record' which you can use to manipulate and cut up the CD (just like a scratch DJ, so they say).

Club units tend to come in the form of two players side-by-side (or 'double consoles') many of which aren't that good. If you want to get into CD mixing, it's more advisable to go for a stand-alone unit, although they're not cheap.

When it comes to other digital formats, there are now excellent MP3 mixing systems, incorporating a PC and control console which you plug into your mixer in the usual way. You can get DJ minidisk players (for a price) and DVD players which can play the video of a song as it is playing. The digital arena is generally accepted to be the future and is worth keeping an eye on, but don't sell your turntables just yet.

‖ Disco Mixer

A disco mixer does two things: boosts the signal from your turntable to a higher level (acceptable to a power amplifier) and allows the DJ to mix the turntables and monitor them on headphones. Don't worry too much about the electronic 'pre-amplification' side of things. From the DJ's point of view, the mixer controls the overall volume of everything and that's as much as you need to know. But with dozens of manufacturers touting their very plausible mixers, what should the ideal mixer be able to do?

It depends whether you are a scratch DJ (a 'turntablist') or a more traditional beat-mixing club DJ, although the two do have things in common. Both incorporate channel faders which allow you to introduce tunes (or other sounds) into the mix from two or more sources. The volume level of the turntable entering these channels is controlled by a gain control, usually a knob (a 'pot') above the fader. A pre-fader listen (PFL) switch or switches allow you to select different channels to monitor in the headphones, which should have an independent volume controller.

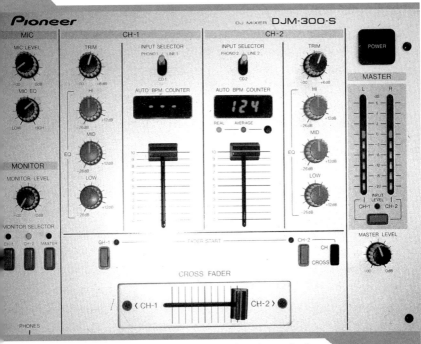

Figure 3: A typical 2-channel mixer

You can fade between channels with the 'crossfader'. Scratch DJs are more demanding of their crossfaders than beat mixers, who simply use them to fade smoothly from one channel to another. Turntablists, however, need to be able to alter how quick the fade is – from a direct cut to a slow fade, depending on what they are using it for so the crossfader needs to be very quick-moving and fluid. They may want to be able to reverse the fade – so that if they fade from left-to-right, the sound actually fades from right-to-left – in order to perform certain moves. For this, you would need the inexplicably named 'hamster switch'.

TIPS

MAKE SURE YOUR MIXER IS DESIGNED WITH YOUR STYLE OF MIXING IN MIND – ARE YOU A TURNTABLIST OR A BEAT MIXER?

All DJs appreciate clear 'VU meters' (a display of green, yellow and red LED lights which show the volume of either the master output or each channel, depending on your selection) and a master volume fader – ideally not placed on the console where you could accidentally knock it. Whereas hip-hop DJs are usually content with a tone control (an 'EQ') which just affects the master output, a beat-mixing DJ needs to have a 'three-band EQ' (i.e. separate control over bass, mids and treble) on each channel.

When buying a disco mixer make sure the unit is sturdy and well laid-out so that your hands have room to move. Check that the sound is good – mixers do vary in quality – and that the headphone output is good, and loud, so you can still hear what you're doing if you have the mixer in a club. Also make sure that there are at least two outputs (for main system and monitor speaker), and ideally you would hope for phono, quarter-inch jack plug (the standard headphone type), and if possible, XLR outputs (the professional three-pin type). Make sure the switches that choose the input source for each channel move slickly and, if possible, that the crossfader is replaceable, especially if you are a scratch specialist. Also, make sure there is a microphone input – this should be an XLR connection – but try not to let the MC know.

Kill switches allow you to cut out certain parts of the sound (bass, middle-range or treble frequencies) from a channel at the touch of a button, and can be useful. Beat counters tell you the tempo in beats per minute (BPM), which is occasionally useful for studio work but next to useless for mixing – your ears are simply much more accurate.

‖ Headphones

There are two essential qualities you should look for in headphones. They must be loud and they should enclose the ear so that you can shut out the other noise in a club. If you spend any serious money on a pair of 'cans', do make sure that they are well made and have a long, durable lead, which is almost always the first bit to break.

Club amplification is complicated enough that people make a career of it. We are talking here about boxes that boost the signal they receive from the mixer with thousands of watts of power. To give you a rough idea about wattage, a mobile DJ might typically have around 1 or 2 kW of sound. A gig at Wembley Stadium might use 100 kW of sound. As well as boosting the sound with amplifiers, club sound systems commonly include very precise graphic equalizers, compressors and limiters to control the sound and all sorts of other gizmos as well. Thankfully this isn't the DJ's problem.

As the mixer gives out a pre-amplified signal that is louder than a normal HiFi component, when setting your decks and mixer up at home you must be very careful not to turn the level too loud and damage your speakers or amp. As long as you bear that in mind, you can plug into any HiFi amp you fancy – just sticky tape your master fader so it cannot go too loud. For those of you with money coming out of your ears, you can of course buy a power amp for home use and you won't have any worries.

|| Speakers

Speakers in clubs are, as you may have noticed, bigger versions of your HiFi speakers at home. So where your HiFi speakers might have tweeters (small cones) for the high frequencies, and woofers (big cones) for the lower end, in a club, you will often find separate speakers for bass, mid-ranges and treble.

‖ Microphones

This book assumes that you are the kind of DJ who does not see yourself using a microphone, so if you're hoping for a few good lines and tips like 'tell the listeners the time about every 2 seconds', then prepare to be disappointed. You do need to know how to use a mic, though, as you may have to make an announcement, and some MCs just get violent if you don't let them have a go.

TIPS

IF THERE IS A PROBLEM WITH THE SOUND, CHECK EVERY ELEMENT THE SIGNAL PASSES THROUGH, FROM STYLUS TO SPEAKERS, IN SEQUENCE, TO LOCATE THE PROBLEM.

Using one is easy: you simply plug it in and turn the level up. Do make sure that when you turn the level up, you are not standing in front of the speakers as you will create a feedback loop and a horrible (but familiar) electronic shrieking sound will spew from them. If you feel you should buy a mic, look for a reasonably cheap and sturdy one, the kind called a 'dynamic' mic.

‖ Cartridges

There are two types of cartridge: some require a separate fitting bit (attached to the head shell) while others screw

15

directly into the arm of the turntable. The second of these needs no explanation: you just unscrew the head shell and replace it with your new cartridge.

The more traditional cartridges must be screwed into the underside of the head shell. You then have to connect four tiny wires, which project from the head shell, to four equally tiny copper rods at the back of the cartridge. The wires and rods are colour-coded so you can match them up correctly. Be very careful to screw the cartridge into the head shell straight, so the stylus reads the groove of the record accurately – you don't want it to hit the groove at an angle, which will damage both cartridge and vinyl.

TIPS

IF THERE IS A PROBLEM WITH THE STEREO ON ONE DECK (E.G. THE SOUND ISN'T COMING OUT OF BOTH SPEAKERS) THE FOUR CONNECTING WIRES ON THE CARTRIDGE ARE ONE OF THE FIRST THINGS YOU SHOULD CHECK.

Tone-arm Weighting

Although tedious, it's crucial to get the weighting of the tone-arm correct in order for the turntable to work properly.

The stylus needs to be at just the right height, with the right amount of pressure applied, so that it doesn't jump out of the groove when a DJ gets busy. These properties are controlled for the most part with a weight attached to the back of the tone-arm. The further up the tone-arm you push it, the more weight is applied.

To find the right weight setting, let the tone-arm hang by the side of the platter. The weight should be screwed well up the tone-arm for this. Then gradually take weight off until the stylus is hanging at the right height to read the record. Then apply a little more weight, depending on the type of cartridge you use. Each arm comes with a recommended weight setting and the scale on the weight is in grams.

You may find that you need to apply more force on the stylus. You can add more weight, but don't go crazy or your records will become crackly very quickly. Another option is to increase the height of the tone-arm, which increases the 'torque', or force, on the needle. Beware, though, some cartridges like the tone-arm flat for best results.

In an emergency (let's say a full club, at two minutes to midnight, on New Year's Eve and the needle won't stay on the record) you can always tape a five- or one-penny piece to the head shell, although, if you do this long-term you could damage your records.

As a DJ you need to be comfortable with the set-up of all of the kit, if only so you can quickly spot when something is wrong when you're playing out.

‖ Getting the Sound from DJ to Dancefloor

Rigging up a basic DJ set-up is relatively easy. There are not too many connections involved, it's pretty logical and it takes a couple of minutes.

Each deck has a pair of phono leads (sockets allowing you to attach phono plugs) which you link up to one of the pairs of phono inputs at the back of the mixer, red wire to red wire, white to white. Most DJ decks have an earth at the back which must be connected to the earthing (or 'ground') point on the disco mixer to avoid feedback. Similarly any other sound source you want to run through the mixer can be plumbed into 'line' inputs with stereo phono leads. If you are going to use a mic, plug it into the mic socket (usually an XLR). Then take another stereo lead from the main output of your mixer to the main amp and one more from your second output on the mixer to the amp for your monitor speaker. Then connect your amps to the relevant speakers and off you go.

Some set-ups may require a bit more work at the amplification stage, but every sound system is different so reading the manual and taking advice from pros are advisable. For home use, of course, you just take another stereo phono lead from your master output to a 'line' input on the back of your amp (i.e. NOT the 'phono' input). Do be careful, though, not to put too much level into your amp from the mixer as this can damage the speaker.

>> HOW TO WORK CHEAPLY

Getting a cheap but worthwhile home DJ set-up is not easy. The problem is the decks and, to a lesser extent, the mixer. You can buy cheap decks, but on the whole, they tend to be lightweight, plasticy and unresponsive, with platters that are upset by a light breeze. You do need decent turntables. Your best bet for something which represents value for money would probably be second-hand Technics SL 1200/1210s which are famously durable. Look through the newspaper classifieds and the ads in the back of industry magazines and see what you can find. If you do take time to set up your decks right you don't need to buy expensive cartridges. Bottom-of-the-line Stantons will do the trick.

Mixers are not so straightforward. Certain budget mixers – and there are loads of them out there – will do fine to get started. Your best move here is to take the time to listen to the models you are comparing in the shop and check them out hands-on. Again, certain mixers are best found second-hand, such as the classic scratch mixer, the Vestax PMC 05 Pro (now, unbelievably, a discontinued line). Reviews either in the dance music press or on the web can be a good source of information on new products.

TIPS

ON THE WHOLE YOU ARE BEST ADVISED
TO BITE THE BULLET AND SPEND A BIT
MORE MONEY ON PRODUCTS WHICH HAVE
SOME CHANCE OF LONGEVITY; AND WITH
TURNTABLES, QUALITY IS ESSENTIAL.
THIS WILL SAVE YOU MONEY IN THE LONG
TERM, SO DON'T BUY ALL THE KIT ON
IMPULSE. THE ONE EXCEPTION IS
HEADPHONES, WHICH BREAK SO EASILY
THAT YOU MIGHT AS WELL GET ANYTHING
THAT IS REASONABLY CHEAP, COVERS
YOUR EARS AND IS LOUD ENOUGH.

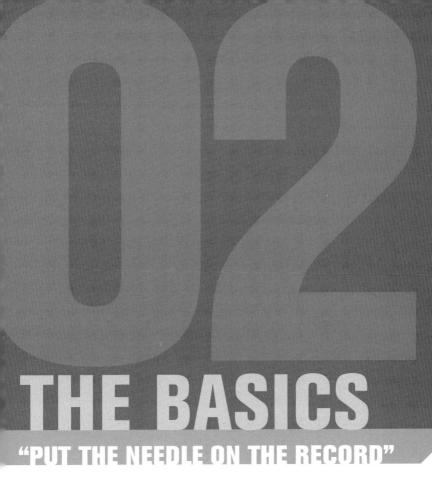

02
THE BASICS
"PUT THE NEEDLE ON THE RECORD"

>> BEATS, BARS & PHRASES

If you don't understand the beats of a dance record, you will have a hard time mixing it.

Luckily, over 99% of dance music conforms to the same basic rhythmic feel – the enormous 1, 2, 3, 4 pounding pulse – that is the familiar boom of the kick drum in a house record. That same pulse is present in R'n'B, drum 'n' bass, hip-hop, Seventies' funk, and more obviously techno and trance along with practically any other modern dance style you can think of (with the possible exception of reggae). If you ever feel that you've lost the beat (it's easier than you'd like to think in a loud breakbeat club) then let yourself nod to the music and you'll find yourself nodding to the beat.

> **There's a fine line between playing records and playing music. If you really don't understand one, you're probably crap at the other.**
> **JOHN DIGWEED**

The reason that the music falls into a 1, 2, 3, 4 pulse is because it is divided up into many smaller units (of four beats each) called 'bars'. In rock or reggae these bars might be made up of various different numbers of beats (depending on the rhythmic mood of the music), however, in dance it is extremely rare to hear music which doesn't correspond to this 1, 2, 3, 4 pulse.

Basic Drum Patterns

Within a single bar of music you will usually hear a number of other drums playing around the main pulse. Figure 4 shows the beats of a typical bar of house music laid out as you might see them when using Steinberg's Cubase, one of the most widely used 'sequencer' music programs for writing house music.

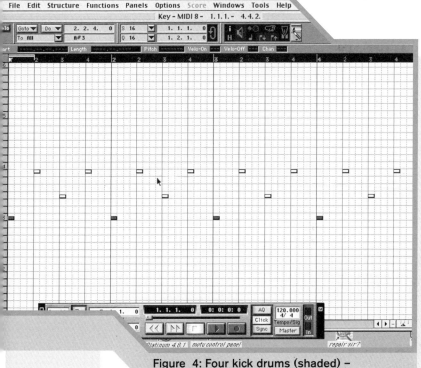

Figure 4: Four kick drums (shaded) –
one on each beat

You can see the main beats of the bar marked (1, 2, 3, 4) at the top of the frame; the kick drum is written in on these beats. In between these main beats, you can see that the screen is divided up by a grid, so that you have four columns making up each full beat. This is because the bar is, in fact, divided up into 'sixteenth notes', or notes so short that sixteen of them fit into every bar.

If you look at the other kinds of drums in the pattern, you can see that the open hi-hat (the cymbal also known as the 'peasoup' because it sounds like that word spoken quickly) falls exactly halfway in-between each pair of kick drums, so that the two patterns in combination divide the bar into 'eighths'. The closed hi-hat (the tiny wisp of air going 'tick-tick' quite fast) usually marks the sixteen sub-divisions in the bar, making the rhythm busier, whilst the snare drum marks the backbeat, falling on the second and fourth beats of the bar.

You could say that the closed hi-hat is the tiny high-pitched noise running fast, the open hi-hat is the slower high-pitched 'psht', the snare drum is the loud thwack, and the kick drum is the low-pitched thundering boom.

The reason all of this is important to you, is that it is much easier to distinguish between the percussion of two different tunes in a mix by listening to their hi-hats and snare patterns than anything else; plus, you will hear when the beats slip out of time quicker if you concentrate on the busy hi-hats rather than the kick drum.

‖ The Music is Divided into Phrases

The bars are grouped regularly in 'phrases'. Rather like a normal conversation, musical phrases are just sentences of music usually lasting about five seconds. Remember, a bar has four beats of the big bass drum, so a four-bar phrase will have sixteen. Try counting sixteen booms of the bass drum in a record a few times in a row and you will soon develop a sense of predicting when the next phrase will begin. The length of a phrase varies depending on the genre of music you listen to, as well as the whims of the producer, but generally there are:

- EIGHT BARS IN A PHRASE IN: HOUSE, TECHNO, TRANCE, US GARAGE, AND....

- FOUR BARS IN A PHRASE IN: R'N'B, HIP-HOP, SEVENTIES DISCO, FUNK.

Drum 'n' base and UK garage tend to vary; often swapping between four-bar and eight-bar phrases and adding a bar in here or there to suit the feel.

This brings us to an unusual, but important, point; whilst 90% of dance records will stick to this rule of phrasing, there are a number of records where producers add in extra bars to get the crowd more excited. For example, in the classic tune by Stardust, 'The Music Sounds Better With You', the music drops to just a solo kick drum twice in the tune – for exactly two bars, or eight booms of the bass drum – before starting back at the beginning of an eight-bar phrase. (And the crowd goes mental every time.) It is important that you know where breaks like this fall, because when you beat mix, as well as getting the beats in time, you need to make sure that the phrasing of the two tunes in the mix is in step, or the mix will sound schizophrenic at best.

TIPS

MAKE SURE YOU UNDERSTAND THE BASIC RHYTHMIC STRUCTURE OF YOUR KIND OF DANCE MUSIC IN TERMS OF BEATS, BARS AND PHRASES.

⊫ Spotting the Beginning of a Phrase

It is not always so easy to hear where the beginning of the new phrase falls, but if you listen carefully to the production of the record, especially the drum programming, you should pick up some clues. There is often a drum fill, or a pause in the rhythm parts, or some sort of 'warning' or 'announcement' in the last bar of the phrase. Occasionally, you will actually hear a record that literally announces the phrases' end by using a sample such as, 'and one more time' or 'le'me hear that again'.

In dance music, especially house, techno and trance, the structure is generally so rigid that new elements are only introduced at the beginning of the phrase, so anytime you hear a new instrument come into the tune, it's odds on that it's the beginning of a new phrase. Over time you will develop that instinctive sense of phrasing so that you always anticipate the beginning of new phrases, but meanwhile it's time to get learning those tunes.

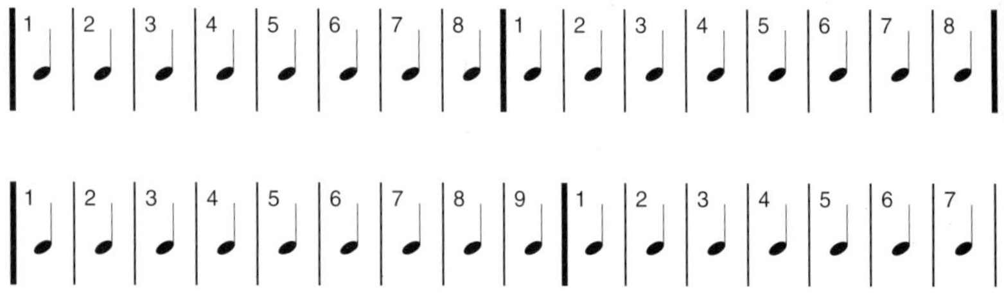

Figure 5: Records with different phras
will not run along happily toget

‖ Beats Per Minute

Leaving aside the structure of the beats for a moment, let's just look at how fast they are. You can measure the speed of a tune in beats per minute (BPM), so this term has come to mean the tempo of a record. It was first introduced when people started using sequencers to make music rather than using live musicians, which meant the timing of most records became tight enough (that is, regular without wavering) for DJs to start beat mixing. With a live band the exact tempo is less of an issue as the human element involved means that timing is less precise.

Here is a rough guide to the range of BPMs of a few common types of dance music:

⊙ R'N'B	80–105	BPM
⊙ HIP-HOP	80–120	BPM
⊙ DISCO	110–135	BPM
⊙ BIG BEAT	90–140	BPM
⊙ US GARAGE	120–132	BPM
⊙ UK GARAGE	125–140	BPM
⊙ HARD HOUSE	130–150	BPM
⊙ TECHNO	130–160	BPM
⊙ TRANCE	140–160	BPM
⊙ DRUM 'N' BASS	160–200	BPM
⊙ BEETHOVEN	WHATEVER	

In practice most DJs tend to play within one style of music, so the tempo of the records they select is roughly similar anyway. Whilst it is possible for the more mathematically-minded DJ to make notes of every record's speed in BPM and work out the correct speed of the next tune to beat mix, for most people the very thought is appalling and in any case, your ears are probably a better and more exact judge of tempo differences than any amount of mental gymnastics.

‖ Trust your Ears

Your ears are certainly a better judge of tempo than any visual reference. Manufacturers dream up devices such as BPM counters, which tend to be added to mixers to make them look good and justify the price. The only times they may come in handy is if you should start to use special effects such as delays, where timing is a crucial factor or you are mixing MP3 files. It is probably more useful for a hip-hop DJ to take notes of BPMs, as there is a much wider range of tempo, although many DJs drop or scratch in the next track anyway, which again makes knowing the BPM academic.

> **[In the DJ booth,] keep your earphones at a low enough volume so as not to drown out the monitors**
>
> **MR C
> (OF THE SHAMEN AND THE END NIGHTCLUB)**

> > GETTING HANDS-ON: BASIC RECORD MANIPULATION

To perform a drop mix, or any type of mixing, you need to be able to get the vinyl to do what you want it to do. You remember how your parents told you never to touch the surface of a record when you were about five years old? Now is the moment to forget all that.

In order to start mixing the first thing you need to do is find the exact moment on the record where you want to bring the new track in. Generally (and always when you are beat mixing) this will be at the beginning of the record – that is, the first beat of the first bar of the tune.

‖ Step One

Turn the power on and put the needle on the record. The easiest way to find the first beat is to let the record play and stop it physically with your hand just after you hear the first beat. Do this by placing your hand on the surface of the record on the opposite side of the vinyl to the tone-arm, holding the record with the pads of your fingertips. This may seem awkward or somehow wrong at first, but you will get used to it in time.

This is where your slipmat comes in handy, as instead of stopping the whole platter, you can hold the record still while the platter is still turning, which gives you much more control. If you try stopping the record in this way without the slipmat, you will find it takes a lot more force and is less exact, because you are fighting the motor of the turntable. In fact, you may strain the motor on some turntables and you will find it is difficult to keep the needle in the groove.

‖ Hands-On

So you're holding the record in place with your hand on the surface of the vinyl, opposite the stylus (see Figure 6).

Figure 6: Cueing up a t

To rewind, move your hand onto the label of the record (do this quickly or you will lose your place) and try to use one hand only, so your other hand is free for the mixer. With your first or second finger, simply wind the record anti-clockwise, making sure you don't press down into the record too hard – you only want the record and slipmat to go backwards; the platter should not even stop, let alone reverse (see Figure 7).

gure 7: Moving a record forwards or backwards

If you find this isn't possible and the whole thing is moving backwards then you are either pressing down too hard, or you need to have a look at your slipmat. Some hip-hop DJs cut out a 12" diameter disc of thin plastic (import record plastic sleeves are ideal) and put it under the slipmat to ensure that it really does slip easily. As you wind the record backwards, you will hear the track play back in reverse. Keep going until you hear that you have passed the first beat – there's usually a tell-tale silence that means you are back at the start of the record – then move your hand back into position flat on the surface of the record, on the side opposite the tone-arm. At first you will find that swapping hand position like this is quite tricky – it's just a case of practice to get up to speed. To make it easier when you are starting out, rewind half a revolution before the first beat. This will buy you time to move your hand from the label back onto the vinyl.

‖ Cueing up

Now that you have found the first beat, make sure that you know exactly where the front of the beat is, physically, on the record. The easiest way to do this is to gently move the record back and forward to give that familiar scratch (or 'wukka-wukka') sound. It won't hurt the record unless you do it in the same spot for hours on end; the needle is designed for this kind of thing. Watch the label of the record as you do this so that you have a point of reference to judge where in the groove that first beat is located. Now you should be ready to let the record play.

If you thought the last bit was fiddly, then brace yourself. Being able to start the record off with your hand so that it plays at the right speed from the moment that you release it is an essential skill for a DJ and the first move in every mix you will ever perform. So this is worth a bit of practice. The more relaxed your hand, the easier this is. The trick is to feel the strength of the motor as you scratch over the first beat. Make sure that you have a couple of centimetres' leeway before the beat, then relax your fingers as you move the record forward, allowing it to move at the speed of the platter, releasing the vinyl at the last moment before the beat, and let it rock.

Figure 8:
Move the record back and forward to give that familiar scratch sound

It probably won't sound amazing the first time you try it, in fact it'll probably be shocking, but you will find even with ten minutes' practice, it will start coming together nicely. For most people this all becomes like second nature within a month or so.

Whilst we're talking about getting hands-on it is worth mentioning how to fast-forward your way through a record. You may find that there are no beats, just ambience, for the first minute of the record, and in a club situation, you don't want to stand around waiting until you get there. So to

Figure 9:
Keep your hand relaxed so as to release it gently and easily

fast-foward, again position your finger on the label of the record and then it is much the same as rewinding with two big differences. This time you need to push down hard into the record to disable the slipmat so that you are in fact pushing the whole platter along; because of the extra weight, you won't find the record slipping and skipping ahead. Try without pushing down into the record and you'll see what I mean. The other big difference, which you may have cottoned on to, is that this time you push the record along in the same direction as the platter is moving.

Figure 10:
Push down hard to fastforward quickly

>> DROP MIXING

Once you have established basic control over the record you are ready to try a drop mix. Drop mixing means to manually bring in a new record, so that the mix does not miss a beat. As well as being a neat, straightforward way of changing the record, it is the first step of every beat mix and, like basic control over the vinyl, is an essential DJ skill. DJs used this technique for years before the dawn of house music and it remains the best technique to use if you're playing disco, funk, Seventies, pop, and is also great for hip-hop and R'n'B, although DJs will also beat mix, where possible, with these last two.

‖ Using the Crossfader

To perform a drop mix, you have to do exactly the same with your right hand as in the previous section: find the first beat

Figure 11: Performing a drop mix

or your chosen start point, cue it up, then release it. This time, however, you need to release the record accurately on the beat – the first beat of the first bar of the phrase, if you have chosen the first beat of the tune – and with your left hand, you need to bring the record in (that is, raise the volume) with the crossfader.

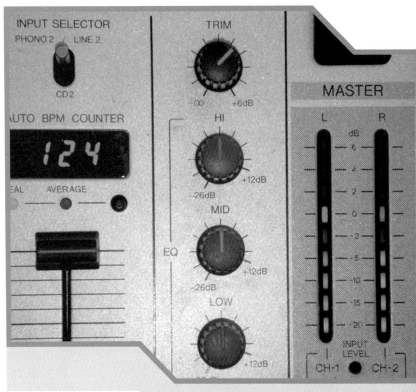

Figure 12: PFL switch

To start with try this without your headphones: when you listen without headphones, leave the fader in the middle. In a club situation, you should monitor the track using your headphones, keeping the crossfader fully over to the side of the record in play and find your start point. You can choose which channel the headphones are monitoring by using the pre-fader listen (PFL) or cue buttons on the mixer. The PFL allows you to hear the track on the selected channel before you bring it into the mix.

Put a record on the other deck. Check that the new tune is at the same volume level. To do this you need to make sure that:

- THE CHANNEL FADER IS AT THE SAME LEVEL FOR BOTH DECKS, AND...

- BY SELECTING BOTH TRACKS, ONE AFTER THE OTHER, WITH THE PFL THAT THE LEVELS ARE THE SAME ON THE VU METER.

However slick the timing of your mix, it will sound terrible unless the level remains constant. You can get away with it at home, but on a loud club system even a small difference is really in your face. If the level drops, then the new tune won't kick, and if you boost it too high, then you'll find yourself in a position where you are left with no headroom to boost quieter records and sooner or later, the level will drop again.

TIPS

REMEMBER TO CHECK THE LEVELS OF THE TWO TUNES ARE THE SAME BEFORE DROPPING THE NEW RECORD IN.

So you've got the levels sorted, you're holding the record at the cue point, in this case the first beat of the first bar of the first phrase of the tune. So when do you bring the new tune in? Think back to the phrasing; you need the first beat of the new record to fall where you expected to hear the first beat of the first bar of the phrase of the record currently playing, so that the music doesn't skip a beat and seems to flow into the new tune, smoothly and logically. Even if there is a change of tempo (which is likely) the crowd will be expecting something new, as it's the beginning of a new phrase. By using the end of one phrase/start of another, or by choosing some other big moment in the music, you will get a bit of camouflage and your mix will be less startling and less obvious.

You will find it easier to make the timing of the mix tighter if you do a little forward scratch over the first beat of each bar, to get your hand in the groove. Then release the record on the first beat of a new phrase, at the same time bring the crossfader over with your other hand, so that you mix out from the old track into the new. Practise a few times, until you are getting the timing exactly right – it's probably best to start with two low tempo tunes; slow hip-hop is ideal.

With time, once you are confident of drop mixing on the first beat of the bar, you can experiment with drop mixing on the upbeat – in other words, just before the beginning of the first bar of the phrase. The same logic applies to this; just make sure that you move into the next record without losing your place in the phrasing. This can be devastatingly effective, especially if you want to smoothly change tempo.

With Seventies' funk or disco records this is almost the only effective method of drop mixing as almost all tracks of that era start on an upbeat, as the drummer gives the rest of the band a rhythmic cue to start playing.

TIPS

PRACTISE DROPPING THE FIRST BEAT OF A TRACK IN UNTIL YOU CONSISTENTLY START THE RECORD AT THE CORRECT SPEED — THIS WILL MAKE DROP MIXING AND BEAT MIXING MUCH EASIER FOR YOU.

03

ADVANCED MIXING

"TWO CARS, TWO LANES"

>> BEAT MIXING

Beat mixing is one of the key elements that makes modern DJs true performers, able to conjure their own sound out of other people's records.

"The most important thing is that you feel your connection to the music. Don't worry about the mixing first; it's what you feel.

If you don't feel it, forget it, don't bother becoming a DJ, 'cos I can tell you there's quite a few DJs out there, who I know, they don't feel it, you can see it. You've got to be in love with it. After that, everything should come naturally,
you know. 🙸

ASHLEY BEADLE

A beat mix is the art of getting two records running together at the same speed with the phrasing of the two corresponding exactly – i.e. when the first beat of the first bar of the phrase in one record is falling together with the first beat of the first bar of the phrase in the other, and so on. While beat mixing may take a bit of practice it is actually fairly straightforward.

There are two ways of beat mixing – using your fingers and using the pitch control (varispeed) – but they are both solutions to the same problem: a problem that is all about acceleration.

Figure 13 is a representation of two records, which are not sitting in time; heard together for a moment we can see which car is ahead, but which is going faster? From this picture alone there is no way of telling. Although the white car is ahead, it is not necessarily moving faster. It may just have started way ahead of the grey car, despite being slower. Similarly, if you hear two records mixed together that are not in time with each other, out of context, it's pretty tricky to work out what's going on.

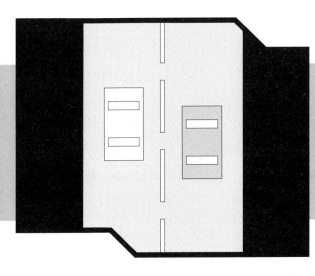

Figure 13:
Two cars,
representing
two records,
where the first
one is ahead
of the second

It is only when you see further pictures of the cars' progress (Figures 14–15) that the situation becomes clearer.

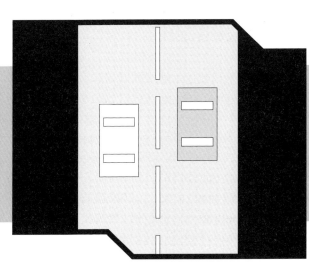

Figure 14:
Now the second
'record' pulls
ahead of the first

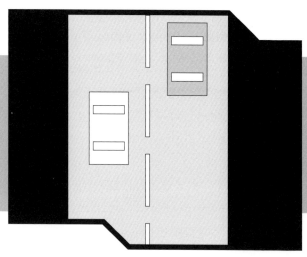

The grey car is overtaking the white car, which is travelling slower, although it was ahead. But how do you work it out with records?

Drop Mixing

It all comes down to the drop mix. If you start the new record by drop mixing it exactly in time with the first beat of the first bar of the phrase on the record playing, then you know for sure that the two records started the phrase at the same time. If they started together it's much easier to tell which tune is going faster, as you can hear it accelerate against the beats of the other record. Plus, you can already start working out how large a difference in speed we are talking about by seeing how quickly the two records go out of time. The quicker they fall out of time, the bigger the gap in tempo. So make sure your drop mixing skills are good, even if you have no intention of ever performing one, and it will make life much easier when you beat mix.

TIPS

STRUCTURE YOUR PRACTICE SESSIONS WHEN YOU ARE LEARNING. START OFF WITH A FEW DROP MIXES TO WARM UP, THEN MOVE ON TO GETTING TWO RECORDS TO STAY IN TIME TOGETHER. ONLY MOVE ON TO COMING SMOOTHLY IN AND OUT OF THE MIX, WHEN YOU ARE CONFIDENT OF KEEPING THE RECORDS IN THE MIX WITHOUT TOO MUCH DIFFICULTY.

To start, try with two copies of the same record at their original speeds. This will give you an idea of how accurate your drop mixing is. Keep trying until it gets tight, note whether you tend to be late in your drop mix or early.

The Two Paths to Enlightenment

There is one basic difference between these two beat mixing methods: whether or not you use your hands on the record or platter to adjust tempo. You will have heard a lot of top DJs use both methods, or a combination of the two, with equal success. A lot of it comes down to personal preference and, to an extent, the style of music that you are spinning.

Most learners gravitate to this technique when they start off and the first step is to look at how to speed up or slow down the record in a controlled way by getting your hands on the vinyl. Obviously this does not adjust the overall speed of the tune, but is useful either after a messy drop mix or when beat mixing in conjunction with the varispeed controller.

> **" If the decks are your first instrument, make sure you can pick up on the start of eight-bar sections. All club music is divided up like this, and if your two records are running in synchronised eight-bar chunks, things will start, stop and fall into place quite naturally. Listen to a tune, and pick out what sound like the natural starting point of sections. If that keeps corresponding with breakdowns or extra rhythm and music coming in, you've got it. "**
>
> **ANDY CATO OF GROOVE ARMADA**

To slow down the record, the trick is to touch the platter, not the record. Let your finger or thumb (use your left hand) brush against the side of the record platter for an instant. It's not complicated: the more pressure that you apply, or the longer that you do it for, the more you slow it down. You shouldn't do this to the record itself, as, because of the slipmat, there's a pretty good chance it'll just stop dead, which is potentially embarrassing. Some DJs squeeze the spindle at the centre of the turntable to slow the record down, which has a more subtle slowing effect, but this method requires a really firm grip on the spindle that lots of people find difficult.

Figure 16: Slowing down the platter manually

When you speed the record up, however, you do need to have your hands on the vinyl. For maximum control, put your finger on the label of the record, pushing down into the platter, to disable the slipmat and move the whole platter. Then move the record on slightly faster, in a clockwise direction taking care to keep applying pressure downwards as well as in a circular motion. If you don't push down, the record will slip ahead because of the slipmat.

Figure 17: Speeding up manua

Make sure that you are comfortable performing these techniques, particularly using your left hand for reasons which will quickly become obvious when you start beat mixing. Again, the best way to get to grips with these techniques initially is to beat mix two copies of the same tune back-to-back (something you can also use as a trick). When you practise, don't use the headphones; leave the crossfader in the middle so you can just concentrate on the deck. Push one record ahead of the other and then bring it back into time and vice versa, until you start getting a feel for the thing. Often when they are almost in time, you will hear the tracks 'phase', meaning that the sound becomes thin and psychedelic. This effect is created by a very slight delay between the two records.

‖ Mixing Two Different Records

When you are happy with your manual control over record and platter you are ready to try and mix two different records together. You can't just beat mix any two records together. They need to be roughly the right tempo and usually of the same genre. So forget any experimental ideas about mixing drum 'n' bass with UK garage. It's probably best to start off with two house records, as the beats tend to be more straightforward. Also look for fairly minimal records or ones with long intros, so you give yourself a good opportunity to do a longer mix. And remember: the better you know your tunes, the quicker you will be able to hear them go out of time, as you will recognise very quickly when the groove does not sound right.

For the time being, don't worry too much about using your headphones. Select the channel you want to listen to on the mixer using the PFL switch and put the 'cans' around your neck, so that you can refer to them if you get confused. To begin with, do the mix with the crossfader in the middle so you can hear both tracks play throughout and just concentrate on your mixing.

Once you're set, drop mix the new record in, starting with the first beat of the first bar of the phrase so it corresponds with the phrasing of the record in play. The two tunes will probably go out of time pretty quickly – what you need to spot is whether the new record is pushing ahead of, or falling behind, the beat. For this example we'll say that the new record is slower than the one already playing and needs speeding up. In this case it is important to do the following:

◉ LISTEN. WHICH RECORD IS MOVING AHEAD? HOW BIG IS THE DIFFERENCE IN TEMPO?

◉ GET HANDS-ON. SPEED UP OR SLOW DOWN THE TRACK AS NECESSARY WITH YOUR LEFT HAND ON THE RECORD/PLATTER.

◉ ADJUST THE VARISPEED. MAKE A CORRESPON-DING VARIATION WITH THE VARISPEED.

◉ TIDY UP (HANDS-ON). MAKE SURE THE BEATS ARE SITTING TIGHTLY TOGETHER WITH YOUR LEFT HAND.

◉ LISTEN AGAIN. WHICH RECORD IS MOVING AHEAD? HOW BIG IS THE DIFFERENCE IN TEMPO?

Do this as many times as is necessary until the records are in time. You need to do this in strict order so that you don't get confused about which hand (the one on the record or the one on the varispeed) is affecting the record. For example, if you push the new record forward it may go marginally ahead of the first tune, whilst still being slower in terms of BPM. If you had moved the varispeed controller at the same time, it would be harder to work out how much the speed needed adjusting.

Drop the record in, check which tune is ahead, make a hands-on adjustment, then a corresponding adjustment with the varispeed (i.e. quicker if you just pushed the record on and vice versa) get hands-on again to get the beats exactly together, so that when you listen, you are starting from a moment when you know for sure that the two records are in time.

" 'In time' is not everything. Two records might be running at the same speed, but with their musical elements clashing horribly. Listen to see if the mix is adding to the moment. If not, keep it simple. Brief cuts which keep the impact of, say, the bassline on the new tune coming in, can be just as effective. **"**

ANDY CATO

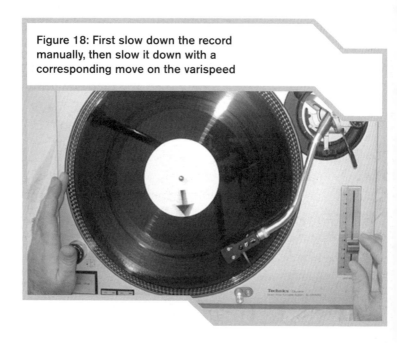

Figure 18: First slow down the record manually, then slow it down with a corresponding move on the varispeed

‖ Make Bold Moves at First

When you make that first move with the varispeed, make it a decent sized move (say +4 if the records went out of time really quickly – perhaps within a bar), gradually adjusting the speed, and do it quickly. The worst that can happen is that you go a bit too far, in which case you will know how to slow the tune down again. Remember, the quicker you get to grips with the speed, the less chance the records have to go badly out of time and the easier you make the task in hand. This also makes you look more slick.

When you are trying to work out which record is ahead, listen to the hi-hats and groove elements like rhythm guitar, congas and so on. These occur more frequently than the kick, so you will notice them go out of time sooner. Also this will help you work out which record is which when they play together – a problem that plagues some beginners. Even if you are confused by the two records in the mix, you can cling on to that one sound and get it to gel into the groove of the other record, so it's worth trying to pick out a groove element that is clearly audible against the other record.

⫴ Using the pitch control (varispeed)

This is a more technical, but probably easier and more reliable method to beat mix (once you get your head around it) and it sounds very smooth indeed. The idea here is to get the two records in time solely by using the varispeed. And it's easy.

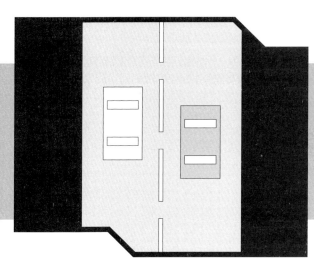

Figure 19:
The grey car is going to have to go faster than the white car in order to catch up

In Figure 19 the grey car is looking to catch up with the white car, then run alongside it – rather like our situation with the two records. In order to do this the grey car is going to have to go faster than the white car in order to catch up. Once alongside the white car it can decelerate a little so as to run alongside. We can apply the same theory to the records. The varispeed on the turntable is like the accelerator.

‖ Too Much, Too Little, Too Early, Too Late

It is not always easy to catch up with the faster record and then fall straight into sync. Using the pitch control slider, the general principle for getting the two tracks in time is to over compensate for each difference in speed. For example, when speeding up the new tune, you would wait not only until the beats had reached the correct tempo, but were beginning to push slightly ahead, then decelerate the track to just below what you thought the real tempo of the tune was, for an instant. Then you would speed the record up to the real pitch, only when you had gone far enough in the other direction so as to make up the difference. In other words, keep going a bit over-the-top (too slow, too fast) until you can finally home-in on the right speed.

In practice, the process will not be a continuous smooth series of reactions and counter-reactions. If, for example you estimated that the record needed to be speeded up to +2 overall, you might accelerate the pitch by +4 or +6 for a bar or so to get the beats to match, before moving the slider back. Typically, you find that over the space of a phrase or two you can gradually home in on the right tempo.

Figure 20 shows the kind of movement this series of speeding up and slowing down actions will give. On the y-axis (vertical scale), you see the pitch-adjustment slider (or, at least, the bit of it between 0 and +6). On the x-axis (horizontal scale), you see the time passing in seconds. The graph shows a series of movements (first up to +5, then down to +3, then up almost as high as +5 again, and so on) to finally end up with a pitch change of +4. Remember though, that all of this has to happen in under five seconds.

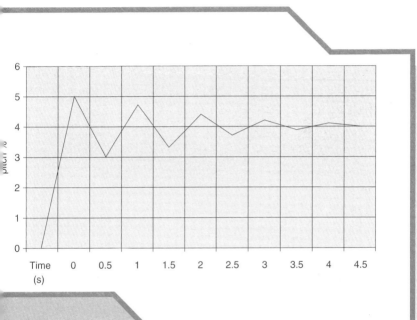

Figure 20: The kind of movement that speeding up and slowing down actions will create

For this method to work, you have to keep your eyes fixed on the pitch-adjustment slider. By tracking your movements against the scale you will soon get a sense of where the correct tempo is likely to fall. After doing this a few times, it becomes a sixth sense. You will have mastered it when you can do it with your eyes closed.

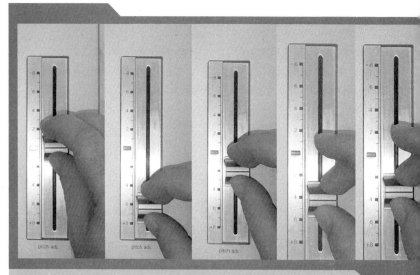

Figure 21: Using the scale on the varispeed as a guide

Remember that the size of your movements is equivalent to how much acceleration you give a car. If you want your car to accelerate fast, you floor the pedal. Similarly, if you need a record to catch up very quickly you can take the pitch-adjustment slider right up to +8, remembering that, as it will probably catch up pretty sharpish, you must also drop back pretty soon. If it takes a long time to catch up at +8, then you know that +8 is not much faster than the correct tempo for the tune – i.e. you will end up with the pitch-adjustment slider near the end of the scale. (If it won't catch up at all, you need to use a more suitable record.)

‖ Coming Out of the Mix

So far we have concentrated on getting the tempos of two tunes to match up. Now we are going to start looking at how to move smoothly from one record to the other, which is, after all, the point of the exercise. If you want the mix to sound natural, then the first thing to concentrate on is the phrasing.

Look at how the dancefloor hears the tracks, assuming that you have got the two records moving in time together, phrase-by-phrase. In house music, the groove is divided into eight-bar phrases. This means that it is difficult to do a smooth mix of fewer than eight bars. This is not the total time you have the two records running together but the total time that they play together in the mix.

Until this point you have used the headphones to drop mix the new tune in (to the phrase) and get the speed right (i.e. as well as selecting the relevant channel to monitor with the PFL, this time you actually put the headphones on over one ear, so you can compare the speeds of the two tunes). The crowd expect new elements to drop in at the beginning of a new phrase, so introduce the new track into the mix at the beginning of a phrase. Then make sure that you drop out of the mix again at the end of a phrase. Try holding two records in the mix for eight, then sixteen, then thirty-two bars and so on. It isn't difficult – you just need to be aware how to bring the track into and out of the mix so that it fits with the phrasing.

It's best to start off by using the crossfader. You'll find that you get the best results by bringing the crossfader across gradually at first, so that the new tune fades in smoothly. Don't be too careful about it; you will hardly hear the new tune if you only nudge the crossfader by a couple of millimetres. To start with, move the fader a quarter of the way across, then slowly bring it over to introduce the new tune at the start of the new phrase. You need to use your own judgment on exactly how quickly to fade and you will find that it depends on both the mixer – a scratch mixer, for example will have a crossfader that may not fade at all – and the style of music you are playing; garage DJs play with the crossfader a lot, swapping from one track to the other, but rarely try to smoothly blend the two tunes.

>> CHOOSING A RECORD TO MIX & READING THE GROOVE

As well as keeping the records in time and the phrasing intact, you will have noticed that some bits of records just don't sit well with others. For example, if you mix two vocal tunes you will get two singers battling for supremacy in the mix, or come out of the mix, cutting off the vocalist mid-sentence, it's going to sound pretty ropey as a rule and very confusing for a crowd who are trying to follow the words. Similarly two very melodic tunes are going to sound like an orchestra at war with itself.

In most dance records there is a drum intro before the main, melodic section kicks in. This has been placed there so that you, the DJ, have a nice sparse, percussive passage to mix into the next tune, before coming out of the mix when the melodic and harmonic elements (basslines, keyboards etc.) come in. So in practice, once you have satisfied yourself that the two records are in time, monitoring on the headphones, it is often a good idea to find the first beat of the drum intro and mix that section over the tune already playing. This helps you avoid clashing melodies and basslines in the mix.

‖ Predicting the Moment

But where do the melodies drop? There are two ways of dealing with this. The best way is to know your records backwards, so you know exactly when the tune drops. But there is another, sneakier way of actually reading the groove on the vinyl so you can work out when the bass is going to kick, or the tune is going to breakdown to reveal the melody.

It's all to do with how the record is cut. Basically the more information that needs to be fitted into the groove, then the deeper the groove. The loudest elements in the record will be the kick drum and the bass. So when the beats drop out, the grooves suddenly become more shallow and tightly spaced.

As a result, these shallow and tightly-packed grooves look lighter in colour and, as you know that the break will start (as usual) on the first beat of the first bar of the phrase, you know to come out of the mix, just as the phrase ends and the needle is coming to this lighter section. This allows you to mix neatly even with tunes you don't know very well. And this is why the light (always the first thing to break on your turntable) is so useful. Without one, in a club, you'll be lucky if you can see the label let alone the grooves.

IT CANNOT BE SAID TOO MANY TIMES: KNOW YOUR RECORDS. THE BETTER YOU KNOW THE GROOVE, THE QUICKER YOU WILL SPOT THE TUNE GOING OUT OF TIME. THE BETTER YOU KNOW THE RECORD'S STRUCTURE, THE EASIER IT WILL BE TO CHOOSE A GOOD MOMENT FOR YOUR MIX.

>> MAKING YOUR MIX SEAMLESS

Levels, EQ and What They Can Do For You

So you can get two records to keep time and you can bring them neatly out of the mix, but it still doesn't sound like Sasha or Oakey. Well don't despair, because so far we've only looked at half the story. As with drop mixing, as well as getting the timing of the two records in the mix to fit together, you also need to make sure the levels stay constant throughout, but as the mix is longer, keeping the volume steady is that much more complicated. The good news is that if you master these techniques you can really start getting creative.

ⅠⅠ Doing Your Level Best

There is a simple law of physics which determines how this works: if you have two sounds in the same place in a tune recorded in stereo, then the louder of the two sounds represents the total output volume until the other sound is within 3 dB (decibels) in volume of the louder element, when the overall volume will increase. Until that point, the quieter sound is hidden behind the louder one. In other words, a loud sound and a soft sound make only a loud volume, but two loud sounds make a very loud volume.

As you have seen, the loudest elements of a dance tune are the kick drum and bottom end bass. These elements are always panned in the middle of the stereo mix. This means that they come out through the right and left channels with equal force and seem to the human ear to be coming from the middle of the two speakers. Pretty much all dance tunes conform to this rule, which is very useful to you, the DJ.

As with drop mixing, you should always check on the VU meters that the new tune is as loud as the previous one before mixing (and do make sure you check how loud it is when the tune is playing, not just in the stripped-down intro section). The big difference with this method is that you don't use the crossfader, you just leave it in the middle, mixing instead with the channel faders. Why? Crossfaders vary in how they work (as we have seen), so you can easily be surprised. Furthermore, even if the crossfader does fade as you want, it is only half the length of the two channel faders; so they give you double the control and you know exactly what blend of the two tunes you have in the mix.

When you first bring the new tune into the mix, bring it in with the fader about half way up (any less than that and, unless the system has studio-clean sound, you won't hear it at all). You can then bring it up to roughly three-quarters of maximum level on the fader, leaving the other channel at its maximum level. From hereon, if you boost the level of the new tune, it should be matched by a corresponding drop in the level of the other channel. Generally you don't need to hear both tracks at exactly the same level in the mix, but if you do want to, they would need to be halfway between this point and the maximum level. Trust your ears and the VU meter to ensure you don't take it too loud.

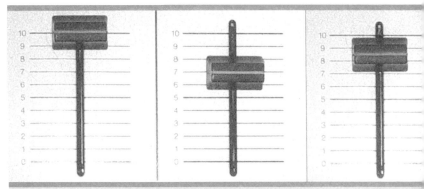

Figure 22: With record 1 at maximum, records 2 and 3 must be set at less than maximum

It must be stressed that these levels are only a rough guide. Remember 'three-quarters' level on one mixer may be 80% on another and so on. So listen carefully when you start mixing to find out at what point the mix seems to bulge and get louder, so you can avoid this problem. You probably want the new track to become the louder of the two at the beginning of a phrase, but if you are mixing trance or more abstract dance, where the mix should sound fluid and organic, a really good smooth fade should do the trick.

Sometimes, as a DJ you find yourself in a situation where you have to run the mixer on full to get enough volume. If this is the case then be very careful with the gain on your channels: you must leave headroom, so that if you come across a quieter track, you can sort the problem out.

Finally, remember to listen to your mix. That means not just concentrating on the next track in your cans, but listening to, and noticing the crowd's reaction. If you as the DJ are lostin your own little world, busily trainspotting with speeds and

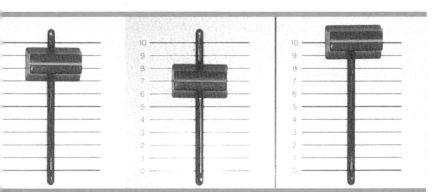

Figure 23: With record 3 at maximum, records 1 and 2 must be dropped in volume

tunes, you are only doing half your job. When you are in the mix, as far as possible, try to get the headphones off your ears – have them around your neck so you can refer to them when confused, by all means – but you need to know what the crowd are hearing if you want to maintain control over the dancefloor and get the most out of your mix.

>> EQ & WHAT IT CAN DO FOR YOU

If you think your mixing's getting pretty smooth now, well, it's about to get smoother. It's important to be able to mix slickly on the faders – you may not have EQ on the mixer you are using in a club, but if you do have the luxury of EQ on each channel, you can take your beat mixing to the next level.

The theory behind this technique is almost exactly the same as with the channel faders. Again you are mostly concerned with the bottom end of the two tunes (i.e. the loud bits such as the kick drum and the bass). But here, instead of adjusting the whole channel level, you adjust only certain frequencies such as bass and, to a lesser extent, mids and trebles.

Again your main concern is making sure that the mix does not bulge, or in more technical terms, that the overall output level or volume remains constant. The way to do it is to use the bass knobs on the EQ to do much the same thing as you used the faders for last time. The difference is that this sounds much more subtle. Not only do you have direct control over the core frequencies of the loudest elements in the mix, but, as these same frequencies are also present in all the other parts of the tune – percussion, vocals, keyboards, or whatever – you are also affecting how present these elements are in the mix. In other words, do this right, and one tune will appear to float right out of the other in a way that can inspire your audience to true DJ worship.

‖ Subtle Use of Bass EQ

When you introduce the new record into the mix, make sure that the bass is down around the 8 or 9 o'clock mark on the tone control knob (the 'pot') while the other channel remains at 12 o'clock, or whatever you have it set to. The channel faders can both be on full from the start – you can use the crossfader if you like – just be careful that the top end doesn't become painfully loud and be prepared to take off a little bit of treble from one of the tunes. Then you are going to bring the bass on the new tune up to 12 o'clock as you take the bass on the other tune out, exchanging one for the other.

Be careful not to start taking bass out of the track you are mixing out of until you have boosted the bass on the new tune enough to avoid the level dropping. Basically, use your ears and make sure the bass stays constant. You may want to go for a very slow, long gradual mix if you are mixing a style that needs to sound organic. If you are mixing more bassline-driven tunes, like funky house, you may well want to swap the basses over in one slick move at the beginning of the new phrase, so you just move smoothly from one bassline into the next; the decision is yours, just let yourself be influenced by the tunes you are mixing. And don't forget to boost those trebles you turned down as the new tune takes the weight.

‖ Creative Use of EQ in the Mix

Once you get into EQ in the mix you can use it creatively in other ways. For example, sometimes the hi-hat patterns of two tunes will not fit together, because one pattern has a swing rhythm, whilst the other is more rigid. Not a problem for you, as you can use the trebles to choose between the two patterns: you can swap them around, as with the bass. You might want to leave two tracks running together so that you get the vocal of one blended with the bass parts of the other or just lose the kick drum for the last bar of the phrase. Thus a whole variety of options are opened up to you.

Of course to be able to manipulate the EQ like this, you need great control over the pitch control, if only because you are going to need to use two hands on the mixer much of the time, but this will come in time. And you will be relieved to hear that for some reason, when you swap the bass parts of two tunes over, for some reason you seem to get away with minor faults in the timing, so this will come together more naturally than you might expect.

TIPS

DO NOT BECOME OVER-RELIANT ON EQ FOR YOUR MIXING. YOU MAY COME ACROSS A CLUB MIXER WHERE YOU DO NOT HAVE CONTROL OVER THE EQ FOR EACH CHANNEL, BUT ONLY THE OVERALL MIX.

04

GETTING SERIOUS

"DOING GIGS & TRICKS"

>> ARRIVING AT THE GIG

Your first move, at the beginning of a set, is to check out how the system sounds and make it sound as good as you possibly can. It may sound obvious but think how many clubs you've been to where the main sound system is distorting and you will realise just how often DJs are unaware of this very basic first step.

When you arrive at the club, take some time out before your set, or during your first record, to stand in the middle of the dancefloor and have a good listen. It's no good relying on what you hear in the DJ booth as the booth will usually be enclosed or located somewhere where the acoustic is quite different, so the main system may sound bass-heavy, lifeless and dull until you get on the dancefloor. Once you have checked the sound, go back to the DJ booth and adjust bass, mids and treble to achieve a good balance. If there is no EQ on the mixer then speak to the manager, or resident sound engineer and get their help to adjust the balance of the sound on the main amplifier. Easy enough, but if you forget, you're going to sound terrible however neat your mixing is.

❝ The sound system is part of the job. Firstly, stand on the dancefloor, and listen. If there's too much treble, mid or bass, remember and correct it when you start. If you arrive somewhere and, as usual, everything's on "11" on the DJ mixer, you've got to make some choices. With no leeway on the volume controls, a lot of tunes that are pressed more quietly [i.e. if there's

more than one track on one side of a record]
will be unplayable. A big tune will not work
if the volume dips by 20% when it comes in.
So pull your loud pressings back and leave
space on the faders for the rest. Or if it's
too late into the night to turn it down, be
realistic. If it's not a loud pressing, your
favourite tune might have to wait for another
night. Watch the meters of the record you're
cueing and match it to the one that's playing.
It's as important a part of a smooth mix
as getting things in time. 🎵🎵

ANDY CATO

‖ Cranking it Up

The other thing to think about is the volume level. A sound
system is much louder when a club is empty than it is when
the dancefloor is full. This is because sound waves are
broken up when they hit people and so lose some of their
impact, whereas in an empty room, they are able to travel
freely until they hit a wall. So you should always keep a bit
of headroom for your master level at the beginning of the
night. No one likes deafeningly loud music early on, when

the club is filling up and people are chatting and drinking at the bar. What's more, if you do start off too loud, you will find yourself in a situation, where, as the dancefloor fills up, the music appears to get quieter and if you've left yourself with no headroom, you won't be able to do anything about it. In any case, in most clubs, you will mostly be concerned with setting an atmosphere until it fills up, so hold back for a while.

The Booth Monitor

The booth monitor isn't just there so that you can turn it right up and pretend not to hear when a punter comes up to you with a particularly awful request. It's also there so that you can monitor the sound coming out of the main system which often appears slightly delayed in comparison to what you can hear on the headphones.

There are two common causes. The main reason is that the signal has to pass through such a length of cable from the mixer to the amplifier(s) and then on to the speakers set about the club, that the sound seems delayed. This means that in a really large club, the speakers at one end of the dancefloor may not even be exactly in time with those at the opposite end. Also, sound will echo off flat surfaces such as walls and these echoes will add to the confusion.

There will usually be a monitor speaker in the booth. Be careful setting the level. It needs to be loud enough so that you can clearly hear the rhythms in the tune, but not so loud as to tire your ears. Once you have sorted out the level, you should set your headphone level, so that it appears marginally quieter than your booth monitor. Most DJs find that this will make it easier to mix in the new tune at the right speed, but you are also avoiding deafening yourself.

A large number of sound systems are set up without a booth monitor, leaving you to cope with the delay on your own. Another thing to bear in mind when you first venture from the decks in your bedroom to a club, is that even a small club system will be a lot louder than you are used to which can be very disorientating.

Always remember to check the obvious things: get the system sounding good, set a sensible level for the sound system, booth monitor and headphones and get ready to rock the house.

TIPS

MAKE SURE THE SOUND SYSTEM OF A CLUB SOUNDS GOOD ON THE DANCE-FLOOR AND DON'T START OFF THE NIGHT PLAYING TOO LOUDLY. STRUCTURE YOUR SET SO IT SUITS THE TIME OF NIGHT AND THE MOOD OF THE CLUB. EVEN A FULL-ON TECHNO NIGHT NEEDS TO BUILD IN INTENSITY. IF YOU ARE ON FIRST, SAVE YOUR MOST BANGING RECORDS FOR WHEN THE CLUB IS REALLY GOING OFF.

There are a few ways you can set the dancefloor alight by showing off.

‖ A Cappella Mixing

Mixing an a cappella vocal over another tune is much the same as doing a conventional beat mix but with a few important differences.

The main difference being that you use an 'a cappella' on one deck (i.e. a vocal which has been pressed onto a record on its own, with no accompaniment). The trick here is that you will mix the a cappella over the top of another record, putting the vocal into a new context. You must therefore choose the record you mix your a cappella over carefully, to make sure that the vocal sits with the other track reasonably harmoniously.

If the vocal is out of tune with the track underneath the mix will sound terrible. In contrast a mix that cleverly puts a vocal into a new musical context can send the dancefloor wild – or even be the basis for writing a tune in the studio. So choosing the right backing track is a big deal and it's worth spending time going through possible tunes until you find something suitable.

Mixing in an A cappella

Once you have a good instrumental to go with your vocal, you then need to mix it. The good news is that, as there are no beats on an a cappella, you have a greater margin of error than in a normal beat mix before the two tunes will

TIPS

THE ORIGINAL MIX OF THE DANCEFLOOR
CLASSIC, 'YOU GOT THE LOVE' BY THE
SOURCE FEATURING CANDI STATON WAS
A BOOTLEG OF THE CANDI STATON A
CAPELLA OVER A FRANKIE KNUCKLES TUNE
'YOUR LOVE'. TRY TO THINK OF SIMILAR
COMBINATIONS TO CREATE YOUR OWN,
NEW RECORD.

sound out of time although, needless to say, you should always aim to keep the mix tight. The bad news is that most vocals do NOT start on the first beat of the bar so you must take care to drop the a cappella in on the right beat. Generally the easiest way to find the right beat is to listen to where the vocal starts in the original mix of the tune, as even if you can't work the timing out, the original producer will have got it sorted. Then it's just a matter of counting as you listen, so you can work out which beat you have to drop mix the a cappella in on.

From hereon in, the procedure is much the same as a normal beat mix. If you have to change the speed of the acapella during the mix (and you will), it's advisable to just use the pitch control, rather than getting hands-on with the record, except in passages where the vocal is silent. You do not want to hear violent changes in pitch in a vocal, as it will sound as if you are strangling the singer, so stick to the varispeed. If you do find that you need to either dramatically slow or speed up the a cappella, then do it in a gap in the vocal, in between words, or verses, to avoid that giveaway squawking diva sound.

As you will see, it is hard to be as exact with tempos as you have no beats on an a cappella. However, you should still be aware of the groove in a vocal, and try to bring it out in your mix. Listen carefully not only to how the singer starts each word or phrase, but also to the endings of words, and you will get a decent feel of where the groove in the vocal is, which will help you mix in time.

‖ Phasing and Back-to-Back Mixing

This trick is done using two copies of the same record, plus they must be two of the easiest ways of impressing your audience.

Phasing

This is a trick you can do with two copies of the same record, which makes it sound as if the song is 'flanging' or phasing (a kind of metallic 'whooshing' effect over the top of the tune), because you intentionally create a tiny delay between the two tracks.

You need to listen carefully to one copy of the record while looking through the groove so you can see which part of the groove corresponds to which bit of the tune – this is best done before the gig. Then you can identify a section that you want to drop in on.

TIPS

PASSAGES WITH LOTS OF TOP-END
PERCUSSION ARE OFTEN GOOD BECAUSE
METALWORK PHASES PARTICULARLY WELL.

Match the tempo of the two decks. Play one copy of the record, whilst cueing up the second copy at the moment you have identified as your drop-in point. Then when the copy playing reaches the start point for the mix, drop the second copy in onto the first beat of the relevant phrase, as usual. Nudge the track into exact time manually, then bring it into the mix at the beginning of the next phrase, slowing it down gradually with your finger as you do so. You should hear a 'flanging' effect over the track. If it is not happening, check if you can hear double kick drum beats. If so, the two records need a smaller delay between the two of them, so again alter the speed manually. If only the bass drum is phasing (unlikely) then you have managed to get the two tracks almost dead in time, and you need to create a slightly longer delay. In practice what this comes down to is alternately slightly pushing on, then slowing down the record until the two tunes really start phasing properly and you hear a metallic, vocoder-like effect.

Back-to-Back Mixing

In comparison to phasing, back-to-back mixing is less

subtle and more likely to be noticed by the crowd given that you add in extra drum beats with the crossfader.

Basically the idea here is that you get two copies of the same track playing back-to-back half a beat apart, allowing you to cut in extra beats from the second copy with the crossfader. Again you need to identify a 'drop in' point much as you did with the phasing, as you need to mix the same passage of the record on both decks. Using the head-phones, drop mix in the second copy of the tune at the rel-evant point and get it in time. Then monitoring both tracks on the PFL, gradually slow down the second copy of the tune until it is exactly half a beat behind the first copy, so that you hear eight kick drums per bar at double tempo, evenly spaced.

Now you can cut in extra kick drums with a swift move of the crossfader, so that they fall on the half-beat between the drums of the main tune, always returning the crossfader for the next kick drum of the first copy of the tune. It is vital that you do not lose the main 1, 2, 3, 4 pulse from the first copy, as you will lose the crowd (who are all dancing to that beat). You can make life easier for yourself by counting along with the main beat in your head, adding 'and' in between each beat, e.g. '1 and 2 and 3 and 4 and'. The 'ands' fall on the half beat, which is exactly where you want to add in the extra kick drums from the second copy of the tune. To do this trick cleanly use of the crossfader needs to be quick and precise, using it almost as a switch to select new beats from the second copy of the tune, before returning briskly to the next beat in the first copy. It may take time to get this right but once you have the knack you won't lose it.

>> CLASSIC TRICKS

‖ Line/Phono Switch Tricks

The line/phono switch controls whether a channel on the mixer receives its signal from the phono input, where your turntable is plumbed in, or the line input, where you might plug in a CD player, tape or DAT machine, for example. Usually if you are DJing largely from records, there is no signal coming into the line input, so if you change to 'line', you will hear silence. This allows you to make rhythms with the track on that channel, by toggling the line in/phono switch quickly and rhythmically. This is particularly effective on a cappella vocals, as it allows you to imitate the effect of 'gated vocals', a pretty cool sound.

Another useful trick is to use the line/phono switch to isolate the kick drums in the mix. (You may find this easier using the channel fader.) Toggle the switch so that it is only in the 'phono' position on the kick drum beats (the 1, 2, 3, 4 in house). Then try making other rhythms with the track. It normally works best on a long drum passage, allowing you to make the bare essentials of your mix more exciting for the crowd by creating new rhythms.

There are a couple of things you will have to get your head around to get this sounding really good. First, you need to get your hand to move fast enough to make for really interesting gated effects. Basically, unless you are quick, you will be limited in your choice of rhythms. The best technique is to use your thumb as a spring and tap out a rhythm with the first or second finger.

Once you have got your speed up, you need to move the switch so that it is in the phono position on the beat. This means that you will have to make your initial movement to the line-in position just before the beat. (If you think about it, your first move is always to the line-in position, as the switch must already be in the phono position for you to hear the tune.) This offbeat movement takes a bit of getting used to, as your natural tendency is to move on the pulse.

It is worth remembering that you can achieve the same effect with the channel faders, although you may not achieve the same speed of movement. On the other hand you may find you can achieve greater control with the faders, particularly when it comes to isolating the kick drum. Make sure you are familiar with how the faders work as once in a club, you may find that the line-in/phono switches are dirty and make a nasty crackle when moved, or are too stiff to move at any useful speed.

Fills and Using the Crossfader

Another way of spicing up your mix, which is particularly popular with the UK garage community, is cutting in and out from one tune into the other while you are in the mix: chopping and changing instead of trying to fade gracefully from one to the other. Back in the days of rave in the early Nineties, British DJs used to cut up the then popular breakbeat rave tunes in this style. A common trick is to swap with the crossfader to the record you are about to mix just for the last bar of a phrase, before dropping back into the original tune. In other words, use the new record to create a kind of drum fill that will introduce the next phrase.

Of course you can swap bars throughout the phrase, especially when you take the trouble to create a pattern which fits in with the phrasing. Good garage and breakbeat DJs will also bring in beats from the other tune within the bar to make up new beat patterns: you have full artistic license to explore this to your heart's content. It depends on what records you play and how good your sense of rhythm and co-ordination are. There's not much more to it than that.

‖ Spinbacks

When you think garage, reggae or drum 'n' bass you think 'rewind!' and no rewind would be complete without a spinback. It's also a good bit of showing off. With a spinback your audience will know that you were in the mix, thus enhancing your rating.

On the last beat of the last bar of the phrase when you are about to come out of the mix, spin the record back sharply on the slipmat. Then crossfade out of the mix on the first beat of the next bar, so you get 1, 2, 3, spin and out into the new tune. You will find that some records work better than others when it comes to spinbacks – and some won't work at all. If the hole in the middle of the record is too tight, try enalrging the hole in the vinyl slightly. But if the record is warped don't try it at all as there's a good chance that the stylus will fly off the record.

Of course if you really want to get the full-on effect, then there's nothing for it but to turn the power off whilst the record is still playing out so that the tune slowly grinds to a halt. Then slowly at first, rewind the tune, still over the system, speeding it up until you take it out of the mix, quickly stop the record, put the needle at the top of the tune, turn the power back on and rock the tune again.

⊩ Mixing with Three Decks

Mixing with three decks is extremely difficult. To reach the same standard as Derrick Carter or Carl Cox you will need to devote a serious amount of time to your three decks, not to mention having some talent. You also need to get your head around monitoring three channels at once, be able to swap between three records quickly and you'll need to know your records backwards. So by all means have a go: it uses exactly the same principles as with two-deck beat mixing, but with another record as well – and that opens up a lot of possibilities.

TIPS

DJ TRICKS ARE A BIT LIKE A GOOD JOKE – THEY DON'T NECESSARILY GET BETTER THROUGH REPETITION. GET YOUR TECHNIQUE SPARKLING AND CERTAINLY ORNAMENT YOUR SET WITH THE OCCASIONAL PIECE OF DAZZLING TECHNICAL TRICKERY, BUT REMEMBER, YOUR KEY TASK IS TO KEEP PLAYING THE RECORD THAT BEST SUITS THE MOMENT.

■

In the meantime, here are some good, slightly easier ideas that you can realistically hope to achieve using three decks, as and when you get the chance.

You can combine a back-to-back mix with an a cappella mix easily. Find two copies of a tune that goes really well with a strong a cappella. Mix them in back-to-back so you can bring in extra beats from the second copy; they shouldn't go out of time as they are the same record playing at the same speed, although unless they are both calibrated perfectly, no two varispeeds are exactly the same. Once you have two copies of the backing track going, with one hand on the crossfader you can add in the occasional beat to get the tune rocking. In the meantime you can sort out the speed of the a cappella on the headphones, then drop it into the mix, allowing you to do rhythmic tricks with the two instrumentals underneath the vocal and send the crowd bananas. It's perfectly do-able. Work on the back-to-back mix and the a cappella mix a lot and you should find you can do it.

The classic use of the third deck is simpler still. You can use it to play bits of movie soundtrack dialogue, sound effects and maybe scratch a little. This can allow you to get creative with all kinds of odd sound bites – enabling you to theme your whole set with the atmosphere of a movie, or maybe just add in a few loops that you are really fond of. There's not much more to add, as this is really a case of letting your imagination run wild – ideally in a large record shop with a full wallet – or pillaging your childhood record collection for choice *Thomas the Tank Engine* moments.

> > **If they don't like your records, do som** tricks. If they don't like your tricks play some records. If they don't like your records or your tricks, you probably won't get paid. **> >**

BT

> > *SERIOUS SCRATCHING*

Scratch DJ-ing (or 'turntablism') is a culture in itself but here is a brief introduction to some of the basic scratches. Before you start off, though, make sure that your slipmat is really slipping, and if necessary, cut out a 12" diameter disc of thin plastic – plastic record sleeves are ideal – and insert it between the platter and the slipmat.

FACTS

- IN 1973 KOOL HERC USED TWO COPIES OF THE SAME RECORD TO KEEP THE BEATS FROM THE DRUM BREAK IN THE MIDDLE GOING FOR LONGER. IN DOING SO HE COINED THE PHRASE 'BREAKBEAT'.

- IN 1977 GRAND WIZARD THEODORE INVENTED THE SCRATCH BY MOVING A RECORD BACK AND FORTH AND FORTH AND BACK TO KEEP REPEATING THE SAME BIT OF SOUND.

‖ The Babyscratch

The babyscratch (the classic 'wukka-wukka') is the building block for all other scratching. It simply involves moving the record back and forth under the stylus to the beat. You can scratch any rhythm you like, as long as it's funky. Try getting control by doing one scratch on the first beat of the bar, then one on every beat in the bar and so on, slowly building the intensity of the scratching movement. You need to keep your hand well away from the stylus. It's also a good idea to start off with a low tempo tune on the other deck, so you won't need to scratch too fast. Do take care to get used to what kind of rhythms work for you at different tempos.

Lots of sounds are good for this – any percussion you can think of, voices, stabs, synth tones. Try this with with both hands, as well as varying the speed that you move the record at to change the tone of the scratch. Basically, although this is the most basic of scratches, it is also one of the most used.

‖ Basic Cutting, the 'Rub' and the 'Stab'

Once you are making some funky sounds with the record, you can look to start using the mixer to sharpen your scratches. The first thing to master is using your turntable as a sampler, dropping in a sound neatly and precisely. This technique is known as 'cutting' or 'forward'.

It is much like a drop mix, except that you are best advised to use the channel fader to bring in the sound. As you release your record, your hand needs to move with it, so that when you pull the channel fader back down to cut off the sound, you are ready, in position, to rewind the record a quarter turn or so, and drop the sample in again. Your fingertips should stay above exactly the same patch of vinyl, throughout the manoeuvre. You may find this easier if you mark the label of the record with an arrow, pointing towards the front end of the sample, so you can see exactly where you are in the tune.

To get speed up, practise this as a series of four movements:

1 PUSH THE CHANNEL FADER UP	3 PULL THE CHANNEL FADER BACK DOWN
2 PLAY THE SAMPLE	4 REWIND THE SAMPLE

In practice, the gaps between these movements are minute. As you get your speed up, you will find both hands move almost simultaneously, but the gaps are still present, so you still drop the sample cleanly.

If you change the order of these movements slightly, you can isolate the pullback as you rewind the record: i.e. play the sample backwards.

1 PULL THE CHANNEL FADER DOWN	3 PUSH CHANNEL FADER BACK UP AND
2 PLAY THE SAMPLE	4 REWIND THE SAMPLE

Now try experimenting with keeping your hand on the record as you push it forwards. This allows you to speed up or slow down the sample with your hand. When you slow

The Cockpit: DJs have to know all the gear, including various makes of turntables, mixers, effect boxes, CD players and computers playing MPEGs

In Action: DJs now feature at many traditional musical events including outdoor music festivals such as Knebworth

Captains of Industry: The Ministry of Sound rose
through the '90s with its flagship club and record label,
to become a major player in the dance music industry

King of the Hill: DJ Carl Cox, a pioneer of advanc
DJ skills and three-deck mixing, consistently featu
in the top ten of DJs (© Andy Cantillon)

DJ Lottie: As just one of a host of talented and respected UK DJs, Lottie is now internationally well-known (© Corey Hart at Black Ink)

Head DJ: Surrounded by the tools of the trade, Orlando teaches DJ skills at Point-Blank in the London DJ studio

Making Records: After years of mixing and remixing other artists' tunes, DJs now frequently make their own records and have become popstars in their own right

On the Job: DJs such as New York's Todd Terry play the top clubs in the UK and all around the world

down the sample, either backwards or forwards as it plays to give a 'deceleration' effect this is called a 'rub'.

The opposite of a rub is a 'stab'. This is exactly the same as a cut, except that you keep your hand on the record and push forward as the sound is in the mix, giving the sound a high-pitched, almost shrieking quality. Again you get a different sound quality if you play the sample backwards.

These are pretty much all the basic scratches. After this you need to get into moves which require far more coordination between the movements of record and faders or switches on the mixer, but their place is in a book dedicated to scratching. However, there is one more basic technique you need to understand, as it was central to the birth of hip-hop.

‖ Beat Juggling: The Loop

The roots of beat juggling lie in that simple 'looping' technique that DJ Kool Herc came up with in the early Seventies. You need two copies of the same record, ideally instrumental hip-hop, although, anything low tempo will do, if you don't mind sounding a bit eccentric.

Again you should mark your records with an arrow on the label so you can find the front of the passage – without using headphones. (hip-hop DJs have all sorts of cunning ways of marking their records so the needle falls straight onto the required beats.) Find an easy passage from the front of a record to practise with.

Cue up the two copies at the front of the passage. Push the crossfader over to the left deck and let the record play. As soon as the passage has finished, drop mix in the first beat of the second copy, crossfading straight into it and immediately rewinding the first copy of the tune to the start of the break, so that you are ready to start again each time a phrase ends. Start with a relatively long passage so that you are not flustered trying to rewind quickly enough, then when you are up-to-speed, move onto a two-bar phrase and so on. In fact this is much easier than you might think – it's really just a whole bunch of drop mixes in a row – as long as you keep a calm, cool head.

Of course on records these days, sampling technology has mostly replaced this technique; only dedicated turntablists and stylish DJ performers still use it. But if you only use it for the occasional flourish, it will add a spice to your set that helps to set you apart from the pack.

05

DIGITAL MIXING

"HIGH TECH & MY DECK"

>> CD DJING & DVD MIXING

CD mixing is a growth area. Over the last ten years, it has become common to see specialist DJ CD players in the DJ booth. But why? There are obvious drawbacks: you can't put your hand on a spinning CD to manipulate it and you can't buy half the tracks you want in CD format. Yet manufacturers are falling over themselves to bring new specialist CD players for DJs onto the market and coming up with ever braver innovations.

While CDs may not have been to all underground DJs' tastes, the mobile DJ and 'Ritzy Club'-style DJ have been using CD consoles for ages. They need to cater for more varied audiences and so have to take a huge range of music to their gigs. As CDs are lighter than records and each CD can take over 70 minutes of music, for them there is really no contest. Mixing is less of a concern for these guys; as long as everyone is dancing, they don't care.

The underground community caught up with CD technology in the late Nineties as CD burners suddenly became more affordable. Until this point if you had just finished a tune and wanted to hear it played out in a club, then you would have had to get an acetate cut. An acetate is much softer than vinyl and can only be played a limited number of times. Getting an acetate cut is an expensive process that involves going to a specialist cutting room. In comparison you can cut a CD at home and the blanks are cheap.

As manufacturers have caught up with this demand, so their designs have become more sophisticated, moving away from the console-type Dual CD-player, bewilderingly favoured in many clubs, to the more professional stand-alone units.

TIPS

MAKE SURE YOU CAN AT LEAST PLAY A TUNE ON A DJ-STYLE CD PLAYER, AS THEY ARE BECOMING A COMMON FEATURE IN MANY CLUBS.

> > TECHNIQUE

Let's go back to basics for a moment. What is different about mixing with CDs in terms of technique? The biggest difference is the interface. Where you can manipulate records with your hand to find, say, a cue point, with a CD player cueing up is different altogether.

Most machines have two modes for cueing up, automatic and manual. In auto mode the player will automatically stop just a split-second (usually a frame, of which there are 75 frames per second) ahead of the first sound on the track. This is great for any situation where you don't have to mix, but less than ideal for beat mixing or rhythmic drop mixing as the first sound of a track is often not the first beat. However, it is great for warm-up applications. Some manufacturers have systems whereby two CD players play one track each continuously, or alternately off two CDs, allowing the lazy DJ to provide ambience without being anywhere near the DJ booth.

Cueing up the CD manually has more in common with (the music production technique of) sampling a record. This is because using either a 'jog wheel' (a huge rotary controller), backwards/forwards buttons or whatever means of control you have available – different manufacturers have come up with variations on this theme – you will find the exact point just before the first beat, to the nearest frame. You then set this as your cue point, usually with a cue button. This makes drop mixing easy as you just have to hit play on the beat as you bring the crossfader over.

If you are cueing up the first beat of the first bar of a phrase, you will need to recognise exactly what the 'attack' of a drum sound sounds like. The 'attack' is the initial percussive impact of a drum sound, such as the 'puh!' just before or at the boom of a kick drum. At normal speed you would hardly be aware of the different parts of the sound, but when scratching or cueing up a tune digitally, you will be able to listen your way through the component parts of a sound such as a drum hit.

CDs also enable you to imitate a vinyl DJ's technique. Some new machines can set multiple cue points in a track, allowing you to set your creatively-chosen cue points in addition to a point to start your mix from. By using the play and re-cue functions on your player you can then cut these excerpts into your mix.

ǁ Cueing Up

As for beat mixing, it is just the same as with records (by using the pitch-adjustment slider) with the exception that the initial drop mix is as described above. Some manufacturers have now introduced a record-shaped interface which allows you to control the CD as if it were a record, but this is really more to encourage scratching rather than to get DJs mixing exactly as they would on vinyl. All the same, it is a major development in DJ technology, as it means that old-school vinyl now has real competition from digital media.

ǁ Looping

As well as this new ability to replicate the immediacy of vinyl, the latest DJ CD players can boast digital tricks, which are relatively new to the DJ's repertoire. Because of the nature of cueing the track on CD, it has been relatively simple for CD manufacturers to expand on this aspect and make a looping function. If you set 'loop in' and 'loop out' points then the player just plays that segment of track. It's a lot easier than making a loop with two copies of the same record – if much less flash in performance terms. This allows you to play your own edit of a song spontaneously – perhaps finding a favourite section of beats to mix under other tunes, a vocal loop or whatever takes your fancy.

DJ CD players were the first format that allowed DJs to change the speed of a track, without changing the pitch of the instrumentation, meaning you could speed up vocal tunes to the max without the singer sounding like they were breathing helium. This feature (now also featured on some digital turntables) means that suddenly you can make greater changes in tempo with the pitch-adjustment slider, giving the DJ more scope to blend styles. Furthermore, in this way you can also speed up or slow down tunes, as they play, with only the most sober dancers even noticing.

In brief, once the sound has been digitally encoded, then as studio technology shows, the sky's the limit as far as playing with sounds is concerned. These new generation CD players are pointing to a new, digital future but, how long will the CD last?

There is already competition in the market place from the DVD. DJs can play songs and videos off DVD. It may not be good for your credibility, but for bars and clubs with occasional dancing, it's an attractive option. Like karaoke, DVD doesn't really fit the brief here. Real DJs don't use that stuff. The real competition for CDs in the digital arena is much more formidable.

MP3 Files

In 1999, you'll remember, the now-defunct Napster introduced the world to PC-based music. MP3 files, however, have in fact been around since 1992. They are basically just a compressed digital file of audio data. And it is the first music format that physically doesn't really exist as a recognisable object. They are revolutionary as they are ten to twenty times smaller than the kind of audio file you find on CDs, and so are a convenient file size for sending via the internet. It worries the music industry for just that reason. Their abstract nature makes it very hard to keep tabs on them and that means the major labels could – and probably do – lose money as a result, as tech-friendly punters exchange them for nothing.

From a DJ's point of view they are the most exciting development for years. They are much lighter than a record bag and there are now various MP3 mixing software/hardware packages available, which are being lapped up by innovative DJs around the globe.

So why are MP3s so good? Well for a start you can still get a lot of good MP3 tunes, free on the web. There are whole sites dedicated to swapping and rating tunes that are pre-released. The systems for mixing are getting better: they can even match the speeds of tracks for you, making beat mixing much easier. And one hard drive can hold thousands and thousands of tunes – just type in the name of the tune you want and there it is with pre-saved cue points.

" The undertaker is coming to measure up my vinyl. "

NICKY HOLLOWAY, DELIGHTED WITH HIS NEW VISIOSONIC MP3 MIXING SYSTEM.

You can control the mix via a disco mixer (as usual), whilst operating the MP3 players either from a computer keyboard or a Dual CD-style console. This allows you to cue up and play tracks just as you would a CD on a DJ CD deck. You will find that you use the pitch-adjustment slightly differently. MP3 mixing software such as the Visiosonic package will calculate the correct speed for the new record for you. But beware: your drop mix is still subject to human error, plus the computer only calculates the speed to a few decimal places so you will have to make minor adjustments, but it's still a lot easier than beat mixing in the more traditional style. Another great feature is that you can swap between tracks faster than on practically any other system. To select the tune in the first place you just run through the computer directory and click – just like finding a document on a computer – and once you have selected a track, you find yourself already cued up, ready to go.

It enables you to continually edit all your tracks. You can save twenty cue points in each track, allowing you to jump in between sections of the tune or create loops with ease. This opens the way for a totally new style of DJing, borrowing from the editing and remixing culture.

There have (predictably) been murmurs of discontent about the poorer sound quality of MP3s and it's true that they are not CD standard. But there is a strong argument that, because certain frequencies have been left out, they actually sound better over a sound system.

Of course, there are drawbacks such as having to copy all of your favourite records, CDs, DATs onto MP3, which is time consuming. Plus, at the moment, you have to take a computer to the club and set it up before the club opens. Nevertheless in a world where you can buy MP3 players the size of bits of chewing gum, hope springs eternal. After all, there was a time when clubs didn't even have varispeed decks.

II Virtual Decks

Virtual decks allow the DJ to manipulate the audio file via a record-type interface or touch pad. As yet this technology is in its infancy, but there are already some good, workable systems on the market and it's only a matter of time before virtual turntable interfaces become indistinguishable in quality from the real thing. So keep your eye out for new developments.

>> HOT MIXING: FX & SYNTHS

The advances in digital technology have also blurred the lines between DJ and studio techniques. There was always a bit of cross pollination – DJs start making loops, sound engineers perfect them with sampling, that kind of thing – but kit that originated in the recording studio is now finding its way into DJ booths.

It all started back in the Eighties with hip-hop DJs using drum machines to sharpen up their sets. This style was known as hot mixing. By the late Eighties acts like Adamski were playing keyboards live over house music. But whilst dance acts used this gear live on stage, DJs left it well alone – the drum machines sounded basic, and keyboards weren't very accessible. However, various effects (FX) boxes and sound modules have come onto the market since.

TIPS

THERE IS ALWAYS A LOT OF GREAT CUTTING EDGE DJ GEAR BEING DEVELOPED. HISTORY SHOWS THAT IT IS NOT ALWAYS THE BEST SYSTEM THAT CONQUERS THE MARKET-PLACE. REMEMBER – IT'S THE SYSTEM THAT YOU WILL FIND IN MOST CLUBS THAT YOU NEED TO BE FAMILIAR WITH.

FX boxes are again not a new DJ tool. Dub reggae DJs have used them for ages. They allow you to add FX to a record such as delays, phasing, reverb and filtering. There are many other FX out there and they can sound amazing.

Here are some common effects:

- ⊙ DELAY MAKES TIMED ECHOES OF SELECTED ELEMENTS IN THE TRACK;

- ⊙ REVERB ADDS THE AMBIENCE OF A ROOM OR SPACE TO THE MIX;

- ⊙ PHASING GIVES A WHOOSHY METALLIC FLANG-ING EFFECT;

- ⊙ FILTERING (ALSO KNOWN AS THE ACID EFFECT) ALLOWS YOU TO FILTER OUT CERTAIN FREQUENCIES FROM THE ENVELOPE OF THE SOUND, WHILE ADDING A RESONANT QUALITY — VERY SPACEY;

- ⊙ GATING INVOLVES CUTTING THE TRACK UP TO PRODUCE A RHYTHMIC STACCATO EFFECT;

- ⊙ DE-TUNING CHANGES THE MUSICAL PITCH OF THE TRACK;

- ⊙ DISTORTION ADDS A GRUNGY LAWNMOWER-LIKE EFFECT TO THE SOUND OF THE RECORD.

There are two possible stumbling blocks when using FX. First, you need to pick your records carefully. In general, FX will sound really effective over the top of stripped down, abstract musical styles where it is easy for the DJ to identify and effect individual sounds. However, with more heavily produced music, you will find that the track is already chock-a-block with sounds, harmonies and effects, and frankly you are best advised to leave the mix as it is.

The other problem with using FX is altogether more simple: as with hot mixing, you really need a third hand if you are going to be able to mix records in quickly and slickly, AND add effects. Again, MP3 could be the solution. You don't have to worry about sorting out tempos – the PC does it for you – so you have more time to mess about with FX and other modules.

TIPS

WHEN USING EFFECTS, USE THEM SPAR-
INGLY – YOUR RECORD SELECTION IS
MORE IMPORTANT THAN YOUR 'FLANGE'.

■

You can now buy dedicated DJ FX units as well as top-of-the-range mixers which incorporate this kind of FX processing. If you are looking into these models bear in mind that you will need to be able to access FX at speed. So, for instance, you don't want to have to manually set a delay time – it takes too long while you are trying to DJ. You need a box that will read the tempo and then allow you to set what kind of rhythm the delay should take at the touch of a button, say a quarter of a beat, or a sixteenth, whatever it may be. Similarly the layout of the unit is important. The controls must be easily accessible, as an overcrowded control panel is not going to lend itself to being used at speed in a live situation.

The final point is noise. Cheap and cheerful FX units will add extra unwanted hiss and white noise into your mix. This isn't such a big issue for home use – although it won't enhance the sound of your mix recordings – but it is obviously something you want to avoid on a loud sound system.

Luckily, manufacturers are increasingly aware of these issues and are also coming up with units that combine FX and loopmaking to allow a DJ to introduce new vibes into their sets. Many of these units combine onboard sounds and loops with the ability to take samples from your own music as well as some full-on digital FX. With the more sophisticated models you can pre-program a whole tune or several. This is all going to take some pre-gig preparation, but the results can be stunning. It's worth checking out a few manufacturers if you are looking to buy, as the onboard sounds on different machines favour different genres, hip-hop, R'n'B, trance, techno, and so on. You will also find that some models demand much more programming and a greater understanding of how to put a track together, so you need to shop around to find a box that suits your needs.

PART TWO

THE DJ BUSINESS

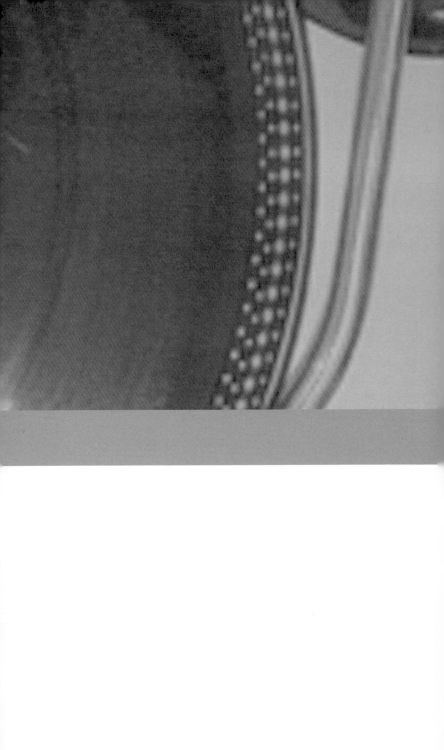

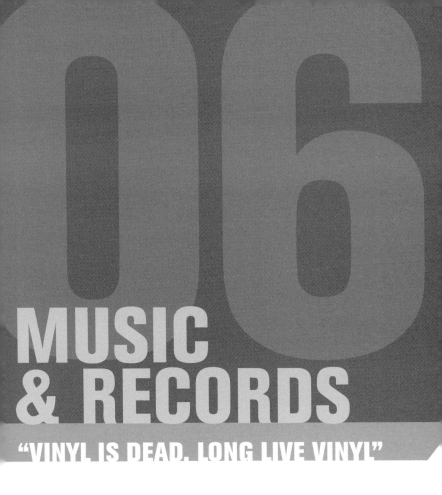

06

MUSIC
& RECORDS

"VINYL IS DEAD, LONG LIVE VINYL"

>> WHY DJS LOVE VINYL

For most DJs there is no substitute for records. They are desirable objects, the sleeves look cool and they have a kind of sound quality you don't get with digital formats (see below). Also a lot of smaller labels just don't make CDs. If you want to buy classic house music, perhaps Nu Groove or Strictly Rhythm releases, you'll find it, second-hand, on vinyl, with only a few compilations available on CD.

Vinyl can also be easily manipulated on a turntable, although various digital formats have managed to come up with vinyl interfaces, such as the giant rotary controllers that simulate a 'hands-on' feel. Another characteristic of vinyl is that you can learn to read the grooves of a record to find desired sections. A scratch DJ can physically mark up a record to find the desired cuts and looping points. It's very immediate.

>> BUT ISN'T DIGITAL BETTER?

The new language of music, digital, encodes the sounds as a series of '0's and '1's on a computer disc. The old language, analogue, encodes the sounds as magnetic fields on a tape, or as tiny hills and valleys on vinyl. Digital isn't better, it's different and there are many advantages and disadvantages to both formats.

The first point of this debate is always sound quality, because it's always assumed that CDs boast a better, sort. Again, not better but different. The full range of human hearing, from the low-frequency bass to the high-frequency treble is reproduced by both systems. With analogue there is no problem whatsoever with the low bass, neither theoretically nor practically. In fact some prefer the effect that analogue has on bass: these frequencies are somewhat enhanced by the relatively large storage space given to them on tape and on vinyl. It's true that the high-frequencies are less reliable and more interfered with by surface noise, but (and this is the key point) the upper limit of these sounds is not distinct and this is an advantage. Like the human ear, a vinyl record will slightly alter high-frequency music according to the individual deck and needle, humidity level and temperature, and time of day. This means that a record is slightly different every time it is heard.

The digital system is, of course, based on numbers. The key number is 44,100. This is the number of snapshots taken of the music every second in order to map the sound. Theoretically this would mean that the highest pitch (or frequency) that can be recorded is 22,050, which is higher than human hearing, and therefore the entire sound should be accurately recorded. However, machines are prone to problems when stretched to their limits and the manufacturers know this. Therefore, most CD players use drastic high-frequency filters that abruptly cut off the high frequencies above a certain point. Even if this cut-off point is set at or near the upper limit of the human ear or the actual music, it still means that the horizon of the music (the extent to which the high sounds are reproduced) is a straight line. This accounts for the sterile, dead or dry quality that people first complained of in the early Nineties when they still had their turntables next to their CD players and could make direct comparisons.

TIPS

VINYL IS NOT DEAD. IT IS NOT EVEN REST-
ING, BUT ALIVE AND WELL. DON'T NEGLECT
VINYL IN YOUR DRIVE TO GET MODERN.

It's the music that counts – not the format. Whatever medium you prefer, it doesn't mean a thing if it hasn't got that wicked sequencer feel.

A DJ is never more than the music he chooses to play. Of course, his popularity will also be tied to his chosen music. Even the most skilled DJ is not going to have many fans if he only plays early Eighties-influenced jack beat jungle. On the other hand, a DJ whose brief is too wide will suffer the effects of blandness.

> **Technically, you can be the best DJ in the world, but if you don't have the right records, you might as well play the spoons.**
> **PATRICK FORGE**

The earliest styles of dance music (as we know that term today) were from the Seventies. Kool Herc started an exciting if crude form of hip-hop and the funk bands chop and change their songs to seem equally spontaneous. These Seventies' funk records are now collectively called rare groove and there is a long career for any DJ who searches hard enough to create a serious rare groove collection and learns to mix it.

TIPS

DON'T FORGET THE SOUNDS THAT TURNED YOU ON TO DJING IN THE FIRST PLACE. STAY TRUE TO YOURSELF.

Styles of Dance Music

Acid

Acid house and old skool are, in some ways, the godfathers of today's dance music. These records are musically conventional but conceptually creative. The old acid sounds, dramatic breakdowns and simple but infectious beats are the building blocks of UK dance music.

Ambient

Essentially playing almost anything. Mixing is not really an issue here as many ambient tracks contain sporadic beats or none at all. The kind of tunes that make tripping love-children smile as they stare that thousand yard stare.

Big Beat/Breakbeat

Named after Brighton's Big Beat Boutique, where Fatboy Slim made it famous, this genre has kept the tempo of house, but has the beats, and cut-and-paste sample attitude of old school hip-hop.

Deep House

In the late Eighties Chicago producers invented deep house, that combined soulful vocals and restrained backing tracks with the big, bad, booming house beat. These days deep house means funky, sophisticated, often instrumental house music, forging irresistible grooves from the mellowest, soul-infused sounds.

Disco

Disco records, themselves, do not really form a modern DJ style. The key difference between the old records and the newer Nineties' versions is (at least) that the Seventies' records have very little bass response by today's standards.

Drum 'n' Bass

Drum 'n' bass (D'n'B) is the super-fast, breakbeat-style related to of the British jungle rave scene. The beats are frenetic and song structure can be all over the place, so you need to be on your toes as a DJ. To be a successful D'n'B DJ you need a good selection of the thousands of D'n'B tunes out there plus a lot of attitude.

Hard House

In the last few years producers have resurrected the big and nasty rave synth sounds of the early Nineties, combining them with banging techno-style beats. Younger clubbers love it and if you don't mind the hoover noises, it's a joy to mix.

House and US Garage

House music is probably the most basic and most effective style a beginner DJ could adopt. The beats are very square, very large and very effective. In many ways, classic house music is the international language of dance music. Almost everyone can find at least one house record that they could bear to hear again. The structure of the music is almost always regular and so is a doddle and a joy to mix. The simplicity of the music lends itself to singing over, and many of the best vocal records in dance music are house tracks. Consequently, many of the best a cappella tracks came originally from house records. If you are a newcomer to house music, choose your records carefully as many of the well-worn classics have been hammered to death.

R'n'B

R'n'B is the sound of modern soul, these days fused with hip-hop beats and even raps, giving it that street edge in the best traditions of funk. In the end, though, R'n'B is about beautifully sung, slickly produced songs, so if you choose this style, you need to be a good judge of vocals and melody.

Ragga

Reggae's hard-ass cousin, ragga uses sparse Anglo-Caribbean beats and the distinctive 'toasting' vocals that has influenced many popular styles, whilst retaining its core audience. Ragga can be tough to mix, but pick the right tunes and watch those booties shake.

Rap

Rap can be a tricky genre to deal with as a DJ. The records seldom follow the musical conventions on which the teachings of this book are based, and can often ambush a DJ by changing abruptly or simply stopping at bizarre points in the tune. If you love the records and you know them like the back of your hand, then anything's possible, but beginners should be careful.

Tech House

Minimal techno synth sounds with funky house beats. It's the same as techno really – just a bit slower and less fierce.

Techno

The sound of techno originated in Detroit, combining electro and house. Nowadays techno is pretty underground, although in its heyday in the Nineties, techno rocked the world. Techno is perhaps the most minimal of four-to-the-floor genres and so allows the DJ almost unparalleled creativity.

Trance/Progressive

The psychedelic sound of trance and progressive house originated in continental Europe at the beginning of the Nineties. Relentless pulsing synths have been sending pilled-up clubbers to seventh heaven ever since. Trance is a particularly DJ-friendly genre to mix and is mass market – Ibiza thrives on it. Whether melodic or brutal, the one characteristic most of these tunes share is fast four-to-the-floor beats with rigid, un-swung drum patterns.

UK Garage

UK garage is the sound of modern suburban Britain, mingling soulful vocals with rough D'n'B basslines and a unique swung breakbeat sound. It's great for mixing – especially if you are good with the crossfader, swapping in between tunes as you beat mix. Again, listen to your tunes carefully; they will not all have regular structures.

>> GO WHERE NO MAN HAS GONE BEFORE

As with everything else in life, new always seems better. A DJ should explore new possibilities and through experimentation, find a style representative of their own taste. The most successful DJs will forge a style of his own that becomes his musical trademark. People fanatically follow a good DJ, but they also follow his music.

The only way to find this Nirvana of DJdom is to keep listening. This may mean spending hours and days and weeks in clubs, record shops or in your bedroom, but if you are destined to reach the pinnacle of DJ Heaven, then there is no other way. If hours in your bedroom with only records, decks and cans sounds like a nightmare, well, maybe you should try cricket. More importantly, whatever you choose, stay on the pulse and never let your record box get tired.

" DJs are in the entertainment business, so it's important to have a lot of energy. You've got to love the music and the scene you're in, because that's where you get your enthusiasm and excitement from, and you must never lose that. We have an expression in hip hop: "I'm doing me". That means don't try to be someone else. Do your own thing. **"**

TIM WESTWOOD

TIPS

WORK TO FORGE A STYLE THAT IS
REPRESENTATIVE OF YOUR TASTES
AND ACCESSIBLE TO YOUR AUDIENCE.
REMEMBER, IF THEY DON'T DANCE,
YOU DON'T WORK.

07

INSIDE THE DJ BUSINESS

"AND I GET PAID FOR DOING THIS?"

One of the reasons that DJs are such icons is that they actually get paid for doing something they love. Or, at least, that's the theory.

So you've got the records, your mixing is phenomenal, you can talk music jargon with the best, and you're ready to rock. How then do you achieve the dream lifestyle? This chapter will give you an idea of the commercial side of clubs and the DJ business. It won't automatically make the dream real, but it does show you how the mechanics of the whole thing work.

EVERYBODY WANTS TO BE A DJ, SO IF YOU WANT TO SUCCEED YOU WILL NEED PATIENCE, PERSISTENCE AND PROFESS-IONALISM. YOU WILL ALSO GET A LOT OF HELP FROM SELF-BELIEF, DECENT RECORDS, AND A COPY OF THIS BOOK.

>> THE POWER STRUCTURE

'It's not what you know but who you know' – this is certainly true of the club industry. You can schmooze a long way in the dance industry, but you need to address things in a realistic order. The biggest DJ management companies can book the biggest gigs, but won't be interested in you until you have some kind of marketable profile. So, unless you are already a celebrity of some sort, you are going to have to pay your dues.

It follows then, that it's your most longstanding contacts, your mates, who should be the first people you think of. Make sure they come to your gigs, so that you get a reputation for bringing a crowd (for whom you can often arrange a guest list). You can always network more successfully from a broader base and friends who talk you up can get you a lot of work. You need to think about where you can find work. For pub or bar gigs you can generally talk to the manager of the place and see if there is any interest.

Always leave a CD of a rocking, recent mix at this kind of meeting. When it comes to clubs, you need to know promoters or become one yourself. There are a lot of promoters who are all talk, so you need to be a careful judge of both character and the proposition. For instance, early in the week most venues find it difficult to get crowds, unless they do student nights. So when a promoter tells you he is setting up a wicked Tuesday night for thirty-somethings at a hot venue, pull the reality 'chute: you may get one decent gig out of it, but by the second week they could be struggling to pay you.

At the end of the day there are charlatans and saints in equal measure. But don't be put off: the more you go out to clubs, the more you will meet people associated with the club scene, and like-minded people. You will meet people who work in record and distribution companies, or other club-related industries and it's amazing how many people can help you out.

TIPS

LEARN TO 'TALK THE TALK' – YOU NEED TO BE READY TO NETWORK YOUR WAY INTO THE BOSOM OF CLUB CULTURE, CULTIVATE USEFUL FRIENDSHIPS AND KNOW WHO'S WHO ON THE SCENE. BUT DON'T FORGET TO BE A DECENT PERSON AT THE SAME TIME.

THE DJ INDUSTRY

PROMOTERS. IF YOU CAN WORK TOGETHER WITH A GOOD PROMOTER — I.E. A GOOD AND IMAGINATIVE ORGANISER WHO KNOWS A LOT OF PEOPLE, HE CAN HELP TO GET YOUR CAREER IN MOTION.

MANAGERS. LIKE PROMOTERS, BUT THEY MANAGE ARTISTS AND DJS. TO BE REALLY USEFUL THEY NEED TO HAVE FANTASTIC CONTACTS, SOUND FINANCIAL AND PR SENSE AND NOT TOO MANY OTHER ARTISTS ON THE ROSTER. ALWAYS ASK YOURSELF, IS THIS PERSON WORTH 15-20% OF ALL MY FEES? PROBABLY NOT WORTH HAVING UNTIL LATER ON IN YOUR CAREER.

CLUB MANAGERS. GREAT FOR FREE DRINKS, INTRODUCTIONS TO ANYONE AT THE CLUB, AND OCCASIONALLY FOR DJ WORK. YOU MEET GOOD AND BAD. YOU NEED TO LEARN TO GET ON WITH THIS LOT, AT LEAST PROFESSIONALLY.

RECORD COMPANY PEOPLE. ALMOST ALL OF THEM WILL BE ABLE TO BLAG YOU THE ODD RECORD IF THEY LIKE YOU. MOST INDEPENDENT RECORD LABELS ARE PRETTY SMALL OPERATIONS, WHERE EMPLOYEES DON'T HAVE PRECISELY DEFINED ROLES. AT THE MAJOR LABELS, FUNCTIONS ARE MUCH MORE CLEAR CUT. IT'S NEVER A BAD THING FOR A DJ TO KNOW RECORD COMPANY PERSONNEL.

PR. PUBLIC RELATIONS PEOPLE HELP PROMOTE RECORDS, ARTISTS

OR DJS TO RADIO, TV AND THE PRESS. IF YOU CAN GET THEM TO HELP PROMOTE YOU, DO IT. ALSO, YOUTH CULTURE IS BIG BUSINESS NOW AND PUBLIC RELATIONS PEOPLE LOVE USING CLUB EVENTS TO PROMOTE THEIR OWN CLIENTS. ALWAYS A POTENTIAL SOURCE OF WORK.

DISTRIBUTION. VERY HANDY TO KNOW, AS THEY ACTUALLY GET THE RECORDS FROM THE WAREHOUSE TO THE SHOP. THEY COULD BE A VALUABLE SOURCE OF INFORMATION, OR USEFUL FOR GETTING HOLD OF NEW RECORDS.

PROMOTION. THESE GUYS ARE EMPLOYED TO SEND RECORDS TO DJS AND GAUGE THE DJS' REACTIONS TO HELP RECORD COMPANIES PREDICT WHICH RECORDS WILL BE BIG.

DOORMEN/BOUNCERS. IT IS GOOD TO GET TO KNOW THE FRONT-OF-HOUSE STAFF AT ANY VENUE YOU GO TO A LOT. THEY'LL GET YOU IN QUICK – FREE IF YOU GET TO KNOW THEM WELL – AND MAY HELP YOU OUT IF YOU EVER PLAY THERE AND NEED A LONGER GUEST LIST.

>> THE MONEY

In order to understand the ins and outs of the DJ's working life, look at their working environment. Basically, for most DJs starting out professionally we are talking bars, clubs and sound systems/events companies.

The bigger clubs have now become marketable brands. Ministry of Sound is the most successful example. On the back of the club's 'underground kudos', they have built up the largest independent record label in Europe (whose compilations enjoy worldwide success), a magazine, an internet radio station, and a merchandising line. In fact the company is now more broadly a youth music media brand than a club.

The basic fact is that clubs, generally, make money by charging on the door, selling drinks, and from anything generated by cigarette machines, pool tables, electronic games, and so on. Often the door money is split with a promoter who helps bring in the crucial money-spending element: the punters. Other costs can include security, wholesale drinks, fags, rent and tax. The DJ may be a running cost of the club, but is often paid by the promoter if there is one involved. From the club manager's point of view, the DJ is part of the PR and marketing – a draw to get the public to pay to come in and then stay and drink. In the bigger clubs, DJs have leveraged this position to their favour to earn big money. They are the draw, so they want a larger cut of the money. In smaller clubs you can leverage your value by trying to get your mates to regularly come down and support you.

Of course DJ-fixated clubbers aren't always the biggest spenders at the bar (although go to some clubs in Ibiza and you'll only be able to afford the one drink anyway). This is why a lot of West End clubs in particular want a split with the promoter on the door.

It's not all glamour for the management. In fact there's a lot of tedious organisational stuff that takes up most of their time. While most club managers now understand the importance of good DJs, there are still those who consider the DJ a necessity to keep punters in the club . These are the managers who will only truly be happy when you play a constant stream of crowd-pleasers.

" Don't feel you have to play only one genre of music. Your record selection is part of making your own style. As long as your records fit well together and fit the overall mood of the night – trancey, funky or whatever – then if it makes them dance, it's alright. **"**

JEREMY HEALY

>> SOUND SYSTEMS & EVENTS COMPANIES

The economics of a sound system company are much simpler. You hire out your gear (a large sound system, decks, mixer and maybe some lights). Some sound system companies will offer to provide DJs and other entertainment along with sound, light, venue decoration, catering and so on, often for corporate events and the very rich. This can be an excellent route into learning about how sound and light works in a gig environment and for getting experience of playing to a crowd, even though you may find yourself forced to play a lot of awful music at various posh functions.

The real downside of this kind of work, though, is that it is very physical. You have to take the entire PA to the gig. Then you get to look after the system all night, troubleshooting if anything goes wrong, before packing up, driving it back to the warehouse, unloading it and finally getting to bed. It's tough work and you will find yourself having to stay awake for stupidly long shifts. Some operators invest in extra gear allowing them to install systems in some clubs on a lease arrangement and do several gigs in a night – useful, as most of the work is at weekends. Still, if you can stand the lugging, it can be a good route in, depending on how organised the company is. And, if you know the right people on the party scene and can afford to buy a sound system and employ people to do the donkey work, it can be a nice little earner.

>> THE MOBILE DJ

This is about as unglamourous as it gets. To the mobile DJ mixing skills are somewhat superfluous to requirement; just make sure you have every copy of *Now That's What I Call Music* ever made. Essentially, this is the worst of all worlds, unless you are a 'personality' DJ, who likes talking nonsense, announcing birthdays and making daft witticisms and aspire to be a certain kind of radio jock. For radio, it's great training; you will see the real cross-section of radio listeners in your area in the flesh, and they'll let you know exactly what they like to hear. The downside includes a serious lack of street credibility, lugging gear (again) but this time on your own.

>> HOW MUCH DO DJS EARN?

The range of DJs' earnings is vast. Top DJs can earn silly money: a DJ of Oakenfold's status can earn a substantial six-figure sum annually from just one monthly residency. Add in extra gigs – one or two a week and extra around Christmas and New Year – and he might double that. And that's before you even account for Ibiza. You hear industry tales of DJs who class gigs as 'cars' or 'houses', depending on their fee for the night. Then there are spin-offs, such as DJ compilations (very lucrative), remixing, and doing A&R – i.e. spotting future dance hits and signing them up for a label – or maybe even running the label. There are also radio

TIPS

DON'T QUIT THE DAY JOB UNTIL YOU HAVE PICKED UP A LOT OF STEADY DJ WORK. MOST DJS HAVE OTHER GIGS ON THE SIDE, LIKE A&R FOR LABELS, RADIO WORK, SPONSORSHIP AND SO ON. UNTIL YOU ARE ESTABLISHED AND FAIRLY SECURE, KEEP THE BANK MANAGER ONSIDE AND MAKE SURE YOU HAVE AN INCOME OUTSIDE YOUR DJ WORK.

gigs, although this tends to be better in terms of boosting your exposure than actually earning hard cash.

Of course if you want to make money, it helps to be a serious workaholic. Hard work will get you a long way. Nevertheless, you will need to love what you are doing and very few DJs can earn a living from DJing alone when they start out. So seize every opportunity you can get to gain experience playing to a crowd. If this means pub or bar gigs on little or no money, so be it, as long as you feel it is the right kind of crowd for your selection of tunes.

08

RISING TO THE TOP

"WAVE WHEN YOU GET THERE"

You've read the book and bought the gear. You've mastered the advanced varieties of mixing and you can scratch with the best of them. You've searched high and low to find just the right trousers, and you've written and rehearsed your acceptance speech for DJ of the Year. Clearly, you're more than ready for your first gig.

So, how does a budding superstar DJ get there? Of course there are a few basic shortcuts. But there are also natural hurdles along the way that can easily be avoided if you know how. At this stage, a little bit of inside knowledge can go a long way.

This is your calling card and it is crucial for making an impression. So make sure you get it right.

HOW TO MAKE A DEMO

CHOOSE GOOD TUNES. THE MOST IMPORTANT ASPECT OF YOUR DEMO IS THE MUSIC YOU SELECT. MOST NON-DJS ARE GOING TO NOTICE WHAT YOU PLAY MORE THAN YOUR MIXING. THE MUSIC NEEDS TO FIT THE VIBE OF THE NIGHT THAT THE PROMOTER IS RUNNING, WHILST ALSO BEING TRUE TO YOUR OWN TASTE. THE IDEAL SELECTION FOR MOST PROMOTERS IS ONE THAT REALLY MAKES YOU WANT TO DANCE – IT'S NOT COMPLICATED. DON'T TRY TO MAKE DEMOS IN A STYLE THAT IS NOT YOU AND IF YOU FEEL THAT YOU NEED TO, THEN YOU ARE PROBABLY GOING FOR THE WRONG GIG.

FIT LOTS OF TUNES IN. THIS IS A GENERAL DJ TIP REALLY. IF YOU WANT TO REALLY GET A CROWD GOING, IT OFTEN PAYS TO MIX PRETTY QUICKLY THROUGH YOUR RECORDS AT THE BEGINNING OF YOUR SET, SO THAT YOU CAN TAKE CONTROL OF THE DANCEFLOOR'S DIRECTION AND CREATE A REAL INTENSITY. BASICALLY YOU WANT TO SURPRISE THE CROWD BY CONSISTENTLY BRINGING IN A NEW TUNE, SMOOTHLY, JUST BEFORE THEY EXPECT IT. THE REASON THIS IS REALLY GOOD FOR A MIX DEMO IS THAT THE

VARIETY OF TUNES MEANS YOU WON'T GET BORED OF THE DEMO ON RE-LISTENING. OBVIOUSLY THERE ARE SOME STYLES LIKE TRANCE, WHERE THIS RULE APPLIES TO A LESSER EXTENT, BECAUSE THE TRACKS ARE LONGER AND STRUCTURED IN A WAY THAT TENDS TO MAKE YOU MIX CONVENTIONALLY, OUTRO TO INTRO.

DON'T WORRY ABOUT LITTLE ERRORS. AGAIN, YOU MUST REMEMBER THAT YOUR LISTENER IS NOT LISTENING WITH DJ'S EARS. A PROMOTER MAY OFTEN BE MORE IMPRESSED BY THE WAY YOU LOOK THAN BY YOUR MIXING. UNLESS YOUR MIX IS REALLY BAD, OR YOU TURN THE WRONG RECORD OFF, YOU WILL GET AWAY WITH MOST SMALL ERRORS – EVERYONE BUT YOU IS MORE INTERESTED IN THE TUNES.

SHOW OFF. YOU HAVE TIME TO THINK ABOUT YOUR SONG ORDER FOR A DEMO IN A WAY THAT YOU DON'T WHEN YOU PLAY LIVE. THIS ALLOWS YOU TO CHOOSE MIXES WHERE SONGS ARE IN TUNE, THINK ABOUT SETTING UP A CAPPELLA MIXES, OR OTHER TRICKS. MOST OF ALL YOU CAN STRUCTURE THE DEMO SO IT JUST GETS BETTER, SUCKING THE LISTENER IN; THINK CAREFULLY ABOUT WHAT YOUR FIRST AND LAST TUNES ARE GOING TO BE – THE FIRST MIGHT BE A SIGNATURE NON-DANCE TUNE – AS WELL AS HOW YOU WILL END THE DEMO AND SO ON.

RECORDING LEVELS. KEEPING THE RECORDING LEVEL CONSTANT IS THE MOST IMPORTANT TECHNICAL CONSIDERATION WHEN YOU ARE MAKING YOUR DEMO. SET A SENSIBLE OUTPUT LEVEL FOR

YOUR MIXER, MAKE SURE YOU STAY OUT OF THE RED ON THE OUTPUT LEDS AND FIDDLE WITH THE INPUT VOLUME ON YOUR CHOSEN RECORDING DEVICE, SO THAT IT IS AT OPTIMUM LEVEL. ALWAYS LEAVE A LITTLE HEADROOM, JUST IN CASE YOU GO LOUDER THAN YOU MEAN TO DURING RECORDING. AND KEEP AN EYE ON THE OUTPUT LEVEL THROUGHOUT THE RECORDING PROCESS. A RECORDING THAT GETS QUIETER IS ANNOYING TO LISTEN TO, AND IF YOU GET TOO LOUD YOU CAN END UP WITH DIGITAL DISTORTION ALL OVER YOUR MIX.

MONITOR THE MIX. DO THIS VIA THE CD-BURNER OR WHATEVER RECORDING DEVICE YOU ARE USING, SO THAT IF THERE IS A PROBLEM BETWEEN THE MIXER AND THE RECORDING MEDIUM YOU CAN HEAR IT.

MAKE IT LONG ENOUGH. A DEMO CD SHOULD BE ABOUT 70 MINUTES LONG. YOU DON'T WANT YOUR LISTENERS GOING AWAY FEELING SHORT-CHANGED.

USE CLEAN SOUNDING EQUIPMENT AND DISTRIBUTE THE MIX ON CD. A DUSTY RECORD SOUNDS CRACKLY AND INDISTINCT. A MUFFLED OR HISSY RECORDING JUST DOESN'T ENCOURAGE YOU TO LISTEN.

REGULAR DEMOS. MAKE A DEMO REGULARLY ONCE EVERY ONE OR TWO MONTHS SO YOU ALWAYS HAVE SOMETHING FRESH, FEATURING A FEW TUNES OF THE MOMENT TO GIVE TO PROMOTERS.

TIPS

DON'T GET TOO PRECIOUS ABOUT YOUR
DEMO. REMEMBER THAT NO ONE IS
GOING TO CONDUCT A CRITIQUE OF
YOUR MIXING ABILITY. THEY JUST WANT
TO HEAR SOME GOOD TUNES.

>> STYLISING YOUR DEMO

Once the mix is sorted, you need to give some thought to
the visual presentation of the demo. It's easy to print out
nice looking CD-sized covers – so think about the look –
maybe you can have a recurring logo or typeface that fits
with your name. Don't leave the thing looking anonymous
and blank. You want people to play it.

It is also worth thinking about your own appearance. You
are a performer and everyone is going to look at you.
Promoters will have more faith in you if you look like a DJ –
as will clubbers, who will trust your selection more.

>> DO I NEED A MANAGER?

It's unlikely that you will need a manager or agent early in
your career unless you are ridiculously successful straight
away. Managers probably can't get you a gig that you
couldn't get off your own back anyway. Managers and
agents make their money by taking a percentage of a DJ's
booking fee, so it is only really worth their while to act on
behalf of established DJs with a bankable reputation. A

really good manager, however, will have contacts within the music industry that will help you to get deals for mix compilations and recording work (if that is your bag) as well as being a great source of advice on your career direction, contracts and your PR. For this they take, on average, 15-20% of a DJ's earnings.

You'll hear a lot of stories about dodgy managers ripping off artists and DJs, so you have to have a pretty good under-standing of the business side of what is going on. To an extent this takes care of itself as, to get to a point where you will need a manager, you are going to have to successfully promote yourself and handle your own business dealings as you build your reputation. The financial side is pretty straightforward: you do gigs, you get paid; just try to make sure you don't get ripped off. Financing records, at first, is more difficult as promo companies and departments will be less inclined to send you free records unless they know you are playing out quite a lot and to decent crowds.

> "Of course the music business is full of wankers – the trick is keep going until you find the good people. "

SASHA

>> MAILING LISTS

In terms of your own self-promotion, there is the whole business of schmoozing and distribution of demos to the world at large. As well as this, you can do a lot more to promote yourself within the industry. Send a weekly chart of your top twenty floor-fillers to the key music magazines and any record or promo companies you want to get to send you records. They may not send anything straight away, but persevere and your name will slowly become ingrained in the industry psyche, so that, when you start getting a few gigs, you will be noticed. Make sure your name is on any publicity media like fliers or posters for a night. You can use these to compile a PR folder on your gigs and various DJing feats.

>> RECORDS

Records are what get you into a club. Aside from everything else, you can't get a job without records. While you're saving up for the best gear available, don't forget to budget for tunes. In fact, start by buying every record that you genuinely love – this is essential. By acquiring the records early on, you'll have more time to study them. The technical DJ skills will come in time and continue to improve forever. By practising with these tunes, you'll learn them, and learn to love them more than you ever thought you could. In which case you'll need to buy more.

> **" Compilations are a good way to study the styles of other DJs and check out stuff that you otherwise would never hear – it may be cheating but it's a lot cheaper than clubbing. "**
> **TALL PAUL**

>> FROM THE BEDROOM TO THE DANCEFLOOR

There's no substitute for practice, but don't think that private practice is all you need. Bedroom rehearsal is a good – and necessary – start, but it doesn't teach you everything. DJing is also about people skills. A DJ doesn't just play music; he plays music to an audience.

It's not enough to simply transfer what you do in your bedroom to a club. Of course, it's possible that someone might naturally rise to the occasion and spontaneously know how to handle a huge, sweaty, impatient, inebriated mass of clubbers. More likely, you'll need to cue up a few times. People behave quite differently at their first ever gig, but it's often along the lines of 'terrified and passive', if not downright frozen to the spot.

Check Him Out Now (He's A Soul Funk Brother)

You could do a lot worse than to study other DJs in their native habitat. When you go out spend a lot of time observing the DJs. Note their demeanour and how they deal with the people immediately around them. Check out how they deal with the punters who approach them. Try to get close enough to hear or guess what people are saying to them. How do they deal with the inevitably naff request?

A good DJ is a bit like a priest. They have to say the right things to the whole crowd to inspire and comfort them. To do this you need to watch the crowd and feel their joy and their pain. React to what the crowd is doing and saying and react quickly. Ride them like a wave, by teasing a bit sometimes and then delivering the knockout tune at the peak. Remember that no one can stay in the same gear for too long.

When an individual punter approaches you with a request, you'll need to be friendly and receptive because of what you can learn from him. Maybe he's a mad drunk with appalling taste (in which case you can safely fob him off with a 'haven't got it with me tonight, mate'). On the other hand, even if his request sounds ridiculous at first, it's possible that he could be telling you that your current selections aren't pleasing the crowd.

Many DJs have a physical style that distinguishes them. Some, like Carl Cox, go in for a show of serious skill by three-deck mixing. Some will actually hit the dancefloor themselves during their own set – although this is trickier than you might think and requires a sharp sense of timing to ensure that you're where you should be promptly. One DJ

gained a wild reputation in the early Nineties for actually setting fire to the vinyl as it was playing, thus creating a wicked
crackling sensation as the record slowly warped and buck-
led under the needle (don't try this at home).

> **I think you should never ever give the crowd what they want or expect. If you want a robot, hire one. I think if a promoter books you, they've heard what you do, so they've got to think about who they put you with. If I come on after Fergie or Lisa Lashes playing at 180 BPM, it's difficult. All those old rules or respect, warming the night up, slowly building it to a big crescendo, that's all gone now.**
> **BOY GEORGE**

And don't be late. It's always interesting to see how one DJ
finishes a set and how the next one starts, and this gives you
a chance to check out the sound of the club and the crowd's
mood. You can also pick up on which tunes in the DJ's set
the crowd are going for, and get an understanding of what
tunes you need to play. Plus you will save your promoter
from having a heart attack.

TIPS

LANDING YOUR FIRST GIG

- TAKE ANY AND EVERY GIG ON OFFER, REGARDLESS OF ITS VALUE

- TELL EVERYONE YOU KNOW THAT YOU ARE AVAILABLE

- BE PREPARED TO TRAVEL

- ALWAYS CARRY A DEMO TAPE OR CD

- SPEND YOUR DAYS IN MANY RECORD SHOPS

- SPEND YOUR NIGHTS IN MANY CLUBS

- LEARN FROM YOUR EXPERIENCES AND APPLY IT NEXT TIME

‖ Your Ever-Changing Record Box

When you do finally get a few gigs and you find yourself on a roll and having fun (and maybe making a bit of money), do whatever is necessary to stay fresh. Holding on to it, is certainly easier than making it but it's still difficult. Remember that the clubs and the punters are always looking for the next big thing so stay sharp.

Stick to what you know and what you love, even though this means spending some time in the shade every now and then. If you chop and change too wildly, you'll only undermine your own reputation. DJs that change style tend to be seen as confused and uncommitted. Besides, no one could afford the cost of completely re-tooling their record collection.

'Old' Is The New 'New'

This doesn't mean you can stagnate. A record box shouldn't last more than a month. Crowds need to hear and demand new tunes, but are not adverse to old ones as well. You must react to your audience no matter how fickle or pathetic they might seem. Be wary of the constant proclamations of what's hot on the scene. Even when 'old' tunes are suddenly (and periodically) back in vogue, assume that it's not for long and don't ever let up on your record shopping.

You must, of course, be cutting edge but that also includes raiding your old collection at home from time-to-time. Many DJs never play any record older than three months but remember that new doesn't always mean good. Don't ever let up on listening carefully to the endless flood of new vinyl that is your life.

> **" A DJ's reputation for music will always overshadow his reputation for technique. "**
> **ALLISTER WHITEHEAD**

>> PROMOTING YOUR OWN NIGHT

To be really sure you get that gig, of course, there is no better way than to promote and run the night yourself. This is really hard work but can be profitable and a laugh along the way. As a promoter, your priority is to fill the joint. So the publicity must be spot on and the club not too huge.

Think up a good name for the night. Get your night listed in club magazines and local papers and listings. Get fliers out there – and make the design funky. Post them to friends and try to get a mailing list of friends' friends so your potential market grows. Written messages to personal acquaintances are always effective. Leave fliers in pubs, clubs and shops which the right kind of crowd frequents. Flier nearby bars and friends' parties on the night.

You need to decide on a sensible door policy in terms of payment. All of your friends will want to be on the guest list, but it's unlikely that you can afford this. A good solution is to set a reasonably cheap entry fee and forget about a guest list. Or you can have a paying guest list. Other areas you need to think about are the décor and lighting: projections are a good and cheap way of filling a lot of wall space. Maybe you can sort out some drinks promotions to encourage the punters. Again, you need to find security if the venue has not got its own and a mate to deal with guest list, money-taking and front-of-house.

Lastly you need to sort out the music, DJs who will ideally pull a different crowd to your own, and a sound system if the

135

venue does not have one. Ensure that you all play complementary styles of music. Techno followed by R'n'B is not going to make for happy punters. It is well worth your while to develop a good relationship with a sound hire company to ensure you get decent rates and good service for the sound system. It's an easy two-way relationship where you supply each other with work.

Now all you have to do is smile all night, talk to everyone, DJ like a god, then count the money and pay everyone. Oh, and a bit of luck helps.

TIPS

BE REALISTIC IF YOU PUT ON YOUR OWN PROMOTIONS. DON'T TRY TO START ON TOO LARGE A SCALE, PULL IN OTHER DJS WHO CAN BRING A DIFFERENT CROWD, AND CONCENTRATE ON BUILDING A FUN VIBE AND CORE GROUP OF REGULAR PUNTERS.

PART THREE

THE MUSIC BUSINESS

09

MAKING
HIT RECORDS
AT HOME

"RIGHT HERE, RIGHT NOW, IN MY BEDROOM"

The last few years of chart music have been dominated by the influence of DJ producers, mostly because DJs are in the best position to recognise a good record and avoid the traditional mistakes of indulgent musicians. As a budding DJ producer, exploit these strengths. Study all of your records as you play them. Analyse the structure of the beats. Measure the depth of the bass drum and the crack of the snare drum. Compare different records to find one that might work as a standard reference for you, and then listen to it periodically during your recording and mixing sessions in the studio. By remaining a DJ in the recording studio, you'll have the best chance of success.

>> UNDERSTANDING THE MODERN RECORDING PROCESS

In the old days, making a proper pop record involved a lot of money. As late as 1990, a three-minute single would commonly cost as much as a car to produce. Of course the record company would initially write the cheque, but if the record was a commercial success the band would ultimately pay the enormous costs out of their takings.

Generally the story would run as follows: You would record a rough demo of your song on a cheap tape-recorder and, if the song sounded good enough, it would raise the interest of somebody who smelled easy money and who had a contact at a record company. If the record company liked the song enough, they would sign you to a record deal, and a budget would be allocated for the proper production of the song. Recording would begin, with a producer, at an expensive studio. The five days for recording would inevitably turn into several more days before the whole outfit then retired to a different – and more expensive – studio for the mixing session lasting about two days. So, with thousands spent on studio time and hired extra gear, and more spent on hiring the producer and the specialist mixing engineer, a radio-quality three-minute version of the original demo would appear in your hands.

Not only would the majority of those musicians be unhappy with the final product, but they would be seething with frustration at the lack of input and control with which their own music was recorded. Technology became increasingly responsible for separating artists from their music.

But now it's different.

Computer recording at home gives artists total control over their own music. As a legal fact, if you pay for and own the means of production, then you own the production. This is key to the future of the music business and is a frightening prospect for record companies.

>> THE 'VIRTUAL STUDIO'

The 'virtual studio' is the digital studio inside your computer. With one of the main music applications installed, you would have:

- A MULTI-TRACK RECORDER WITH PERHAPS A HUNDRED OR MORE TRACKS;

- A MIXING DESK WITH PERHAPS A HUNDRED OR MORE CHANNELS AND FADERS;

- A MICROPHONE AND INSTRUMENT PRE-AMPS TO PLUG YOUR OWN GEAR INTO;

- A FULL RANGE OF EFFECTS INCLUDING REVERB, ECHO, DELAYS, COMPRESSION, ETC;

- A 'MASTERING' RECORDER TO RECORD FINAL MIXES AND DO POST-PRODUCTION WORK;

- THE CAPABILITY TO BURN YOUR OWN CDS TO DISTRIBUTE AND SELL.

With not much more than a PC, most people can for a reasonable price own their own facilities to do everything that, until recently, only record companies could do. Welcome to the music business.

>> WHICH HOME STUDIO ROUTE TO TAKE

Home studios are always based around a computer, but that doesn't necessarily mean that no other gear is needed. Broadly, there are three basic routes available to building a studio: Buying software, buying gear and buying a workstation.

‖ Software

This route involves keeping everything inside one computer. This is the most straightforward route and the most popular because it only involves a computer, a keyboard and a few disks. It may be the cheapest option for those who are entirely new to the game and as yet own nothing, because it's possible to cut a lot of corners during your early days by downloading software from the internet.

The disadvantage is that you must learn how to use the software before you can record a single note. Because you are converting what is fundamentally a word processor into a studio, just about everything must be learned from scratch. Of course, it's easy once you know it, but the first few weeks using a new software studio can be tedious and frustrating.

‖ Gear

This is the natural route for people who have attempted a home recording before. If you already own a MIDI keyboard, a drum machine, a synth or a small mixer, then it probably makes sense to use what you've got. This route could still involve many of the same computer programs as the software route, but the key difference is that you could use some sort of connection device (or interface) to connect your old gear to your computer. The advantage is that you'll feel comfortable using the gear you've had for all these years and, therefore, you'll be able to start making sounds much quicker. You may be able to utilise ideas that you started long ago by transferring the old notes straight into your new system. Another advantage is that you will end up with your own personal collection of bits of kit which are entirely unique, and this will almost certainly give you a sound which is totally your own. This quality cannot be over estimated, especially with so many new studios using only the standard computer programs of the moment.

TIPS

IF YOU ALREADY OWN BITS OF RECORD-
ING EQUIPMENT DON'T NEGLECT THEM.
ANY SORT OF INTERFACE WILL GIVE YOU
A UNIQUE COMBINATION WITH WHICH TO
MAKE YOUR UNIQUE SOUND.

■

143

These are self-contained set-ups, comprising a keyboard with lots of presets/sounds, and a built-in recorder on which you just hit record and off you go. Its versatility enables you to set it up almost anywhere – a kitchen table, or back seat of a tour bus. Just plug it in, put on some headphones, press record and start jamming.

This route is by far the best for instant results. In fact, many people find that, on purchasing a workstation, they knock out their first tune on their very first day. This route can also be the cheapest, provided you're willing to work with a somewhat limited (but still quite impressive, mind you) range of possibilities. If you're an absolute beginner this could be an advantage, although limited in technological possibilities it enables you to focus on recording a song.

There are many disadvantages – many people will be working with identical sounds, your choices will be limited, and there is the unavoidable problem of eventually growing out of your chosen workstation, or just getting bored of it.

>> SOUND SOURCES

Whatever route you choose, it's important to begin the whole recording process with a basic understanding of the different sounds that can make up a record. There are five different (basic) categories of sound sources.

‖ Microphones

Sounds which you can hear with your own unassisted ear

can be recorded using a microphone. The most common example is the human voice; singers sing, and rappers rap into a mic. Other examples include acoustic guitars, orchestral instruments such as violins and trumpets, live drum kits and percussion.

All microphones only emit a tiny, weak signal and therefore need to be plugged into a 'mic pre-amp', which boosts the signal up to a strength equal to the other sound sources. When recording with microphones, always remember to set the input channel to 'mic' rather than 'line' or any other setting.

TIPS

IF YOU'VE NEVER USED A MICROPHONE FOR RECORDING, DON'T LEAVE IT TOO LONG BEFORE YOU TRY. MICROPHONES WILL ALWAYS CREATE THE MOST DISTINCTIVE SOUNDS AND MAKE YOUR RECORDS TRULY UNIQUE.

Line-Level

This term encompasses anything that has a plug with which it can be connected straight into a mixing desk. The most common example is the synthesiser. Other examples are electric guitars (non-electric guitars and violins, for example, that have a 'pick-up'), electric pianos and keyboards, and tape machines and CD players. When recording 'line-level' sources, always connect them into channels set to 'line' or 'direct' (not 'mic').

Turntables

Record decks are a special category of their own because they always require their own dedicated pre-amp (as when connected to a DJ mixer) before being recorded as 'line-level'. When recording your own decks, plug the output of the DJ mixer into a 'line' input of the recording mixer whether it is hardware or computer-based.

Samplers

Samplers are, in one sense, just the same as synthesisers in that they put out a 'line-level' signal at the back of the box. They should be considered as a separate entity, however, because they actually contain no sounds in themselves. In order for a sampler to make any sound, you must first 'sample' (that is, record) a sound of your own choosing with it. Thus, the nature of the sampler as a source of sound to record will be entirely dependent on what you choose to sample. If you sample something quietly, the output may be as low as a microphone. If you sample loudly, the output will be a regular line-level signal.

Feedback

While this is not usually a sound that is encountered voluntarily, it should be considered as a sound source in its own right. While we all recognise feedback as the obnoxious whine that screams at us from speakers on occasion, its important to understand what it is. Whenever you connect an output to an input, feedback is born. This may be the act of simply aiming a speaker (the output) into a microphone (the input), or it could happen when you accidentally connect the output wires of any box into its' own input. Although some people actually use feedback as a desired performance sound (as Jimi Hendrix often did), most people seek to avoid it. However it occurs, feedback can be deafening (especially the digital variety) if left unchecked for more than a couple of seconds.

>> MIDI & SYNTHESISERS

Musical Instrument Digital Interface (MIDI) is the electrical code language for musical information. It is an accepted industry standard which all manufacturers employ and the code is always the same. Each note on the keyboard has a number, starting with '1' for the lowest note on the piano (also known as 'C-1') and rising by one number for each note.

As a universal musical code, MIDI allows any two machines to be connected via a MIDI cable (with 5 pins at each end) and to 'talk' music to each other. In practice, this means that, by pressing the notes on one electronic keyboard, a connected machine will respond by sounding the notes as played. More importantly, it means that a performance on a plastic keyboard can be sent and recorded, via MIDI, into a connected computer. Other information, such as preset changes and pitch bend and pedals, can also be communicated.

In Sync and Doubling Up

MIDI is a vital part of the gear-based style of a studio because all the various bits of kit need to connect musically. For example, if you own a drum machine, a MIDI connection would allow you to run it along side (and in sync with) your computer and any other gear in use.

Similarly, any two synthesisers can be combined as one using MIDI to allow the doubling-up of preset sounds. (For example, a piano sound on one synth can be backed with and supported by a string sound on a different synth to create one enormously lush sound from a single performance.)

Many people find that it's easier to sample a synthesiser's sound into your computer and then perform and finalise the part inside the computer, but others prefer the purity of sound that comes from allowing the synth to perform its own sound – via MIDI – live during the final mix.

>> SAMPLING

Most dance music is created through sampling. Endless varieties of textures and various mix-and-match techniques are made possible and whole new genres have grown out of it.

Sampling simply means recording a relatively small snippet of an already-recorded sound and then manipulating that snippet in your own way. Many of the best modern digital synth sounds are created with samples.

One example is a standard grand piano preset sound: the

manufacturer of the synth actually uses a microphone to record a real grand piano playing a selection of single notes, and then creates a program in which each of the recorded single notes is played back whenever the corresponding note on the synth keyboard is pressed. In this way, the 'real' sound of a Steinway piano is heard when the Casio note is played.

TIPS

INSTEAD OF BUYING SYNTHESISERS FOR YOUR SET-UP, SIMPLY VISIT A GEAR-OWNING FRIEND AND SAMPLE SEVERAL NOTES ACROSS THE KEYBOARD ON A PARTICULAR SOUND AND SAVE IT AS A SAMPLED 'PRESET'.

‖ Loops

This is another common example of sampling. A short three-second section of an old vinyl record (usually a drum beat) is sampled and then edited so that it repeats itself without missing a beat or dropping the inherent rhythm. The loop is then assigned to a particular note on the keyboard so that it can be triggered to play (via MIDI) at the desired moment just as if it were a note of a piano in a song.

By changing the speed or the pitch of a chosen loop, or a segment of a different record, dramatic effects can be created which then inspire and create whole new records.

Samplers can either be self-contained boxes like synthesisers or simply computer programs with an added input plug at the back of the computer. The original and still the most popular sampler is the Akai 'S' series which began in 1988 with the 'S-900'. Updated models are available and many have fantastic newfangled features and tricks, but the gist of the process remains the same: Choose a short sound or snippet, sample it, mess around with it.

But Do I Have to Pay Anyone for the Samples I Use?

Legally and officially, the sound of an old record is owned by the record company that produced it. As they own the copyright in the sound recording they must give permission for any use, at any price they choose. Legally, you will only have infringed their copyright if you use a substantial amount of the record but this technicality is a lot more complex than it sounds and it would be unwise to try to outwit the lawyers.

Instead, it's usually a good idea to use the golden rule of basic music economics. That is to say: 'Sample first, ask questions later'.

If you produce your own 12' or CD either as a demo or just to press a few hundred for a specific and short-term reason, then the chances of anyone who cares about your having sampled them ever hearing your record are infinitely small and it seems a bit silly to worry about the repercussions at all.

If you are producing your own 12' or CD and you expect to

press and sell less than 5,000 copies, then, regardless of what you sample, it would hardly be worth the legal fees necessary for anyone to actually sue you. Such a relatively small-scale producer could assume that the risk is negligible and just sample away to his heart's content.

Even if you are producing your own recording with the hopes of it becoming a global hit, then it still seems inappropriate to worry about the offending samples. If you should be lucky enough to land a massive record deal with a major label, then you can be sure that the corporate lawyers will handle it all for you.

Of course, if you're already signed to a record company or management contract then be sure to let them know what you're doing when you do it.

>> USING DJ SKILLS & ATTITUDES IN THE STUDIO

If you've played out as a DJ for any length of time, then you will probably know as well as anyone what makes a great record. You know what sort of BPM works best for certain purposes and you know which breaks and drops can send people into orbit. These nuggets of knowledge are the raw materials of a good record producer.

Of course, you've got to start with a good idea. If you can't think of one, get a partner who's a musician – that usually works. After the idea is fleshed out, however, things can all too easily go wrong.

Obviously, the DJ producer's main advantage is his DJ skill. The perspective of a DJ as a mixer is a unique and valuable one because it's quite different to that of a standard musician. The DJ producer should try to think of the record he's producing just as he would a set he's mixing. Chop and change the arrangement to suit the overall mood as necessary. Drop it, beat it, scratch it and switch it. Do what you do. Play to the crowd.

>> MIXING A RECORD

After you've set up your studio, got a good idea, and recorded all the bits and worked the arrangement to perfection, you've still got to face doing the final mix. Arriving at this point can sometimes be a problem for a DJ producer if he's too used to mixing a different thing every night. Making a lot of unchangeable decisions can seem seriously daunting, but it is something that has to be done.

> **You never finish a record, you just abandon it.**
>
> DAVE STEWART
> OF THE EURYTHMICS ON MUSIC
> PRODUCTION AND MIXING

‖ Putting a record to bed

Be prepared – remember the destination of your final mix. When you decide that your mix is finished, you'll need to record the last play-through of the song as a master final mix onto a tape player, DAT, CD or straight onto your computer's hard drive. By choosing which format to use at the beginning of your mix, you'll be able to watch the levels on the destination machine (or hard drive) from the outset. You can do this by setting it to record and play and pause; thereby seeing the input meters as if you were recording but without actually running. This will also keep you focused on the sound of the mix at the crucial end point rather than having to stop and set up your medium just when you've memorised your mix moves for that final part of the tune.

Try to run all the various devices at their optimum level. While it is technically possible to run all the individual channels and instruments at wildly wrong levels and still get a decent mix if the master level is correct, you'll probably get a better result if you watch your details. In practice, this means starting out the mix session by watching each part run individually to see what sort of peaks and troughs it hits throughout the whole pass of the tune. It's slow and tedious, but you're likely to find at least one or two individual parts that would sound better if their level were re-adjusted either at source, on the channel, or on the fader. Try to get a good compromise between each of the stages of each of the parts in your mix. Run everything as loud as possible but without any unplanned distortion occurring.

Listen to the mix in sections (both kinds). It's amazing how your perspective on a mix changes when you only listen to certain sections of it at a time. First, try listening to the introduction of the song by hitting 'stop' on the first beat of the first verse, several times in a row. Try the same thing with a chorus, bridge, or a breakdown. Listen to the same section each time it occurs, but in quick succession. Compare the first chorus directly to the second chorus. Are they exactly the same? Should they be so? Should one be adjusted to be more powerful than the other? Second, try listening to certain instruments throughout the entire song. Start with the drums and percussion and study them as they play throughout the song without being distracted by the other instruments. Ask yourself whether each part of the drum/percussion section is as clean and powerful as it should be. Then do the same again listening to the keyboards, and then the vocals. Much will be revealed with such close inspection.

Keep changing the speaker situation. If possible, rig up a second pair of speakers in the mix room next to your usual pair, and somehow position a switch just near your chair so that you can select either pair with minimum effort. As often as you can remember, maybe after every single pass of the song, keep switching between the pairs of speakers. Notice the difference in sound on the two pairs. If there are any glaring differences, try to find a compromise in your mix. Mix so that, as far as possible, the tune sounds as good on one pair as it does on the other.

The 'Cassette' Method

If you haven't got or can't manage a second pair of speakers in the mix room, arrange a second pair – no matter how small they may be – in another room. Periodically, maybe every hour or so, make a cassette of the mix as it currently is and go to the other room to see how it sounds. Again, note the differences and adjust accordingly.

A brilliant trick used by many top mixers has been to put a tiny, stereo or ghetto-blaster in the mix room. Try listening through it periodically by using the cassette method described above. Notice how much bass is lost (remembering that quite a bit of bass is supposed to be lost on small speakers) and note which sounds and instruments stick out and which are buried.

TIPS

NEVER MIX FOR MORE THAN A COUPLE OF HOURS WITHOUT LISTENING TO THE MIX ON A DIFFERENT SET OF SPEAKERS.

‖ Listen in MONO

It is always a good idea to listen to your mix in MONO as often as possible. After all, most clubs run everything in mono and, even if they don't, few clubbers ever stand in a position long enough to appreciate stereophonic sound.

And don't forget to physically move around your mix room while listening to the mix. Rooms always have 'sweet spots' and 'dead spots' where the music sounds particularly good or bad. Try to identify these spots and perhaps (carefully and subtly) adjust the mix accordingly.

10

INSIDE THE MUSIC BUSINESS

"FROM DJ TO POPSTAR"

> ### THE NEW ROLE FOR RECORD COMPANIES

Despite the fact that it is now common for a record to make it to number 1 in the UK while only selling a mere 30,000 singles, it's still true that far more records are sold overall now than ever before. And, despite the apparent similarity of style of so many recent chart hits, there is still more variety of music available today than there has ever been before.

New 'shoot low, and hope for the best' attitudes have only recently become practically possible because of the falling costs of recording professionally at home. If a record takes only a week to make and costs less to produce than you make in one gig, then even a modest return is an excellent result and would certainly inspire most people to repeat the exercise.

>> WHAT IS A RECORD LABEL?

Although a record shop could easily make a punter think that the world is full of thousands of different record companies, the reality is that there are – for most intents and purposes – only five. They are:

- BMG (THE GERMAN-BASED BERTELSMAN MUSIC GROUP)

- EMI (THE SOLE ENGLISH PLAYER)

- SEAGRAM / UNIVERSAL (SEVERAL OLD COMPA-NIES ALL NOW OWNED BY A WHISKEY MAKER)

- WARNER (PART OF AOL TIME WARNER)

- SONY (FORMERLY CBS)

As we have seen, record companies don't do much recording anymore. To understand what they do is the modern music business and this level of understanding automatically makes you a player.

Rather than actually recording the artists or producing the records, these companies now deal with distribution, marketing and promotion. It is difficult to generalise about how record labels operate. Some seem to have quite a lot of autonomy to run themselves and make all their own decisions, while others are entirely dominated by their parent companies.

The majority of these thousands of labels have now rationalised themselves in an attempt to adapt to the new game. It has meant reducing or even scrapping all recording budgets to concentrate on signing those artists whose demos are already in a fit state to release. And has also meant re-adjusting attitudes that were previously focused on traditional pop-chart success.

There are so many labels, selling so many records, in so many styles, that an ability to think in non-traditional ways, such as using a niche dance music chart as a launching pad, is as important as any other marketing or selling skill.

>> PACKAGING YOUR DEMO TO SECURE A RECORD DEAL

If you are going to attempt to secure an offer of a record deal, you will need to somehow first attract the label's attention.

Almost all demos are delivered on CD, though cassette is still possible. The main advantage of the CD demo format is that the issue of quality is immediately apparent. If the label wants to hear release-able material, a top-quality CD mix is going to make the point while a cassette will not. Deals are rarely offered on cassette demos and generally only when the music is so good, and so appropriate to a label that they are willing to actively pursue it. A well-designed cover will go some distance towards getting you noticed initially and, with thousands of demos received daily, this is no small point. There is no formula for standing out but originality and innovation are key.

TIPS

IF YOU USE CDS WHEN YOU PLAY OUT, MAKE (OR 'BURN') A CD OF YOUR OWN MUSIC AND TRY IT OUT ON THE CROWD. IF NOT, YOU CAN HAVE YOUR OWN MUSIC 'MASTERED' AND PRESSED AT A MASTER-ING STUDIO FOR ABOUT THE USUAL COST OF THREE OR FOUR NEW WHITE LABELS.

>> YOUR STATUS AS A DJ

Every link in the music business chain has been affected by the rise of the DJ. Record companies, labels, publishers, distributors, record shops and promoters all respect the DJ producer/artist and seek them out. Therefore, being a DJ is an asset and should be exploited at every turn.

Clearly, it's important to let them know you are a DJ straight away. For some, this means calling yourself 'DJ Guy' or something similar but that is not the only way. It may be more appropriate to simply include a biography of yourself, on the cover, that begins with, 'Guy has been a DJ for some years and regularly plays at the hottest clubs' or similar.

Another ploy would be to use a photo, on the cover, perhaps one of you DJing at a club. Make sure it's a good, sharp or otherwise arty photo, and hopefully wild or interesting as well. Alternatively, use a photo of a record deck or some other DJ icon.

TIPS

NEVER PITCH YOUR OWN MUSIC WITHOUT MAKING SURE THAT THE LISTENER KNOWS THAT YOU ARE A DJ. THIS WILL CHANGE THE WAY THE PERSON HEARS THE MUSIC.

>> PROMOTING A RECORD

If a larger label has signed your record and is now to release it, the main job is to promote it.

Records are occasionally advertised in mainstream ways (like TV commercials) but this is relatively rare. The most common method of promotion is simply to get people to actually hear the record. This might be on commercial, or pirate radio, in retail shops, or in clubs. Wherever it is, though, the key is to convince the playlist chooser (known as a 'producer') to play your record. It's not practical or even possible to approach these producers yourself and so you need to use dedicated professionals. The people who do the convincing are called 'promoters'. Everyone needs a promoter. From the major labels to the DIY DJ artist, the right promoter can make the difference between a hit and a miss.

Promoters are generally one-man operations though some agencies do exist and thrive. Their relative success, though, is never based on the scale of operation. Indeed, the biggest hits can be promoted by a one-man band while major labels can employ hugely-expensive agencies only to go completely unnoticed. The whole trade is about word-of-mouth personal relationships – who do you know?

The only way to find a promoter is to ask around. Even if you have no contacts at all, you have to start somewhere. The local clubowner or regional radio station may be your starting point. Failing that, try the other DJs who you play out with.

If at first you don't succeed…

> >  RADIO

As throughout the history of dance music, radio continues to be a key factor in the success or failure of a record. Without some appropriate radio support, even a major label cannot place a hit. On the other hand, a single one-off unexpected play on Radio One has been known to spontaneously generate a hit record.

Radio is generally controlled by the promoters who have the ear of the radio show producers but, occasionally, a radio DJ will take a personal liking to a record and champion it. Therefore, although it's a longshot, it's always worth sending a copy of your record to a radio DJ who you know likes your style of music.

As with record companies, be sure to package the CD so as to appear as professional as possible, and try to catch their eye and ear.

>> DON'T BE PUT OFF

It's true that the music business isn't what it used to be, but that's a good thing for DJs. It means that companies are far more receptive to your ideas than ever before. If you can manage to turn your DJ aptitude into a good tune of your own, the industry is just waiting for you.

There is no limit for a skilled and innovative DJ. Everything is possible: worldwide travel, vast fees for gigs, unrivalled pulling power, hedonistic days and non-stop party-filled nights. DJs have become the gurus and spokespersons for their generation.

As you make your way through the multi-dance floored, and fashion-victim dance club that is all part of life as a DJ, try to be different. Do it for the music and do it for yourself.

" Any way you look at it, DJs make the best records. **"**

DAVE SEAMAN

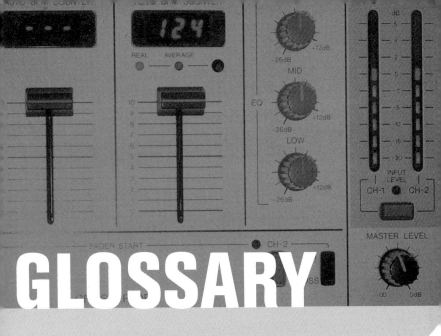

GLOSSARY

A CAPPELLA ITALIAN FOR 'WITHOUT VOCALS'. USUALLY, A 12" MIX WITH ONLY VOCAL PERFORMANCES AND NO MUSICAL ACCOMPANIMENT AT ALL.

ACETATE A DUB PLATE; A TEST PRESSING ON 'ACETATE' WHICH IS SOFTER THAN VINYL AND CAN ONLY BE PLAYED A FEW TIMES, USUALLY USED FOR DEMOS.

BABYSCRATCH THE BASIC ONE-HANDED SCRATCH ('WUKKA-WUKKA').

BACK-TO-BACK MIXING A TECHNIQUE USING TWO COPIES OF THE SAME RECORD, ONE OF WHICH IS HALF A BEAT OR MORE BEHIND THE OTHER, ALLOWING THE DJ TO ADD IN BEATS OR 'ECHO' BEATS.

BAR A SMALL UNIT OF MUSIC USUALLY MADE UP OF FOUR BEATS.

BASS LOW-FREQUENCY SOUNDS SUCH AS THE SOUND OF A BASS DRUM OR A BASS GUITAR.

BASSLINE (OR 'B-LINE') THE LOWEST MELODIC LINE IN A TUNE, TYPICALLY PLAYED ON A BASS GUITAR, OR AS A BASS SYNTH SOUND.

BEAT ONE SINGLE PULSE OF MUSIC. IN HOUSE MUSIC, ONE BASS DRUM PLAYS ON EACH BEAT.

BEAT COUNTER A DEVICE THAT MEASURES THE TEMPO OF A TUNE IN **BPM**.

BEAT JUGGLING A SCRATCH TECHNIQUE WHERE THE DJ MAKES A LOOP OF TWO SECTIONS OFTEN OF IDENTICAL RECORDS, EITHER TO KEEP A BREAK GOING OR TO CREATE NEW RHYTHMS.

BEAT MIXING THE TECHNIQUE OF MIXING TWO RECORDS TOGETHER SO THAT THE BEATS AND PHRASING FALL PERFECTLY IN TIME.

BPM BEATS PER MINUTE; THE TEMPO OR SPEED OF A SONG.

BREAKBEAT THE WORD ORIGINATES FROM THE DAYS OF

EARLY HIP-HOP, WHEN DJS WOULD LOOP THE BEATS FROM THE DRUM BREAKS IN THE MIDDLE OF FUNK RECORDS. THESE BECAME KNOWN AS BREAKBEATS. NOW THE TERM OFTEN APPLIES TO ANY SAMPLED OR LOOPED BEAT THAT HAS BEEN TAKEN FROM ANOTHER TUNE, AS WELL AS BEING USED TO DESCRIBE MUSIC DRIVEN BY THIS KIND OF RHYTHM.

CANS SLANG FOR **HEADPHONES**.

CARTRIDGE HOLDS THE STYLUS ON THE END OF THE TONE-ARM. YOU USUALLY BUY THE CARTRIDGE AND STYLUS TOGETHER AS A COMPLETE UNIT.

CHANNEL A VERTICAL STRIP ON A MIXING DESK, USUALLY HAS A DECK PLUGGED INTO IT, WHICH LEADS TO THE MASTER SECTION AND THE AMPS. THE PATH WHEREBY A SIGNAL IS TRANSMITTED ELECTRONICALLY FROM ONE POINT TO ANOTHER.

CROSSFADER THE FADER THAT ALLOWS YOU TO CHOOSE BETWEEN THE TWO MAIN INPUT SOURCES ON YOUR MIXER.

CUE TO CUE UP A RECORD OR CD IS TO FIND THE START 'CUE' FOR A MIX.

CUT A SCRATCH TECHNIQUE MEANING TO DROP A SOUND INTO THE MIX. IT CAN ALSO MEAN A TUNE OR 'TRACK.'

DECKS ALSO REFERRED TO AS **TURNTABLES**.

DELAY A TECHNIQUE ALLOWING YOU TO MAKE TIMED ECHOES OF SELECTED ELEMENTS IN THE TRACK.

DETUNING CHANGING THE MUSICAL PITCH OF A TRACK.

DISTORTION A GRUNGY LAWNMOWER-LIKE EFFECT ADDED TO THE SOUND OF THE RECORD.

DROP MIXING (AKA GROUND) A TECHNIQUE WHERE YOU SIMPLY DROP A TUNE INTO THE MIX AND SIMULTANE-OUSLY CROSSFADE OUT OF THE PREVIOUS TUNE SO THAT THE MIX DOESN'T MISS A BEAT.

EARTH A WIRE THAT 'EARTHS', OR GROUNDS, AN ELECTRICAL UNIT, ALLOWING UNWANTED ELECTRICITY, LIKE STATIC, TO ESCAPE WITHOUT CREATING NOISE IN YOUR MIX.

EQUALISE (EQ) COMPLEX TONE CONTROL THAT ENABLES THE USER TO ACCURATELY CONTROL A SOUND'S TIMBRAL BALANCE. USUALLY, THE SETTINGS FOR 'TREBLE', 'MIDRANGE' AND 'BASS.'

FADER A SLIDING CONTROLLER, LIKE THE CHANNEL FADERS ON A MIXER.

FILTERING THE 'ACID' EFFECT. A TECHNIQUE WHICH ALLOWS YOU TO FILTER OUT CERTAIN FREQUENCIES FROM THE ENVELOPE OF THE SOUND, WHILE ADDING A RESONANT QUALITY.

FREQUENCY THE NUMBER OF EVENTS IN A GIVEN TIME. FOR EXAMPLE, THE NUMBER OF VIBRATIONS PER SECOND. USUALLY USED IN REFERENCE TO THE RELATIVE 'TREBLE' OR 'BASS' OF A SOUND.

FX (EFFECTS) FX BOXES ALLOW YOU TO ADD EFFECTS SUCH AS DELAY, REVERB AND GATING TO A TRACK.

GATING CUTTING THE TRACK UP TO PRODUCE A RHYTHMIC STACCATO EFFECT.

HEAD SHELL THE EQUIPMENT ON A TURNTABLE THAT CONNECTS TO THE END OF THE TONE-ARM.

HELICOPTER A SCRATCH TRICK WHERE THE DJ SPINS HIMSELF AROUND ON THE TURNTABLE, STANDING ON HIS HAND(S).

HOT MIXING THE TECHNIQUE OF MIXING RECORDS WITH DRUM-MACHINE GENERATED, OR SEQUENCED BEATS.

KILL SWITCH A SWITCH ON A DISCO MIXER, WHICH ALLOWS THE DJ TO MUTE BASS, MID-RANGE OR TREBLE FREQUENCIES.

LINE-IN/PHONO SWITCH INPUT SELECTOR ON ONE CHANNEL OF A DISCO MIXER.

MIDI MUSICAL INSTRUMENT DIGITAL INTERFACE. THE ELECTRICAL CODE LANGUAGE FOR MUSICAL INFORMATION.

MIXER USUALLY REFERRED TO AS A 'DISCO MIXER' IN DJ TERMS; IT PRE-AMPLIFIES THE SIGNAL AND ALLOWS THE DJ TO MERGE DIFFERENT MUSICAL INPUTS.

MP3 A COMPRESSED DIGITAL AUDIO FILE. THE FILES ARE SMALL ENOUGH TO BE SENT EASILY OVER THE INTERNET, AND ARE THE FORMAT FAVOURED FOR PC DJING.

PA USUALLY MEANS THE SOUND SYSTEM; OR, CAN MEAN PUBLIC APPEARANCE (A LIVE ACT).

PFL PRE-FADER LISTEN. THIS ALLOWS YOU TO MONITOR DIFFERENT CHANNELS ON A MIXER. SOMETIMES REFERRED TO AS 'CUE' ON DISCO MIXERS. ON A DJ MIXER THE BUTTON MARKED PFL WILL ALLOW YOU TO MONITOR THE TRACK THAT IT CORRESPONDS TO.

PHASING THE WHOOSHING EFFECT CAUSED BY TWO PARTS OF THE SAME RECORD BEING PLAYED AT EXACTLY THE SAME TIME.

PHRASE A MUSICAL 'SENTENCE' LASTING FOR EITHER FOUR OR EIGHT BARS.

PITCH THE BASIC FREQUENCY OF A SOUND WHICH DETERMINES HOW HIGH OR LOW IT IS, MELODICALLY. IT CAN BE USED TO MEAN 'SPEED' WHEN USING DJ EQUIPMENT, AS IN 'PITCH CONTROL.'

PITCH CONTROL (PITCH-ADJUSTMENT SLIDER, VARISPEED) THE CONTROLLER ON A DJ TURNTABLE FOR ADJUSTING THE TEMPO.

PLATTER THE PART OF THE TURNTABLE THE RECORD RESTS ON.

RAM RANDOM ACCESS MEMORY.

REVERB ADDS THE AMBIENCE OF A ROOM OR SPACE TO THE MIX.

RUB A SCRATCH TECHNIQUE, WHERE YOU KEEP YOUR HAND ON THE RECORD, SLOWING IT DOWN, AS YOU DROP THE SOUND EITHER BACKWARDS, OR FORWARDS, INTO THE MIX.

SAMPLING CAPTURING A SNIPPET OF SOUND FOR MUSICAL MANIPULATION. THE DIGITAL RECORDING OF SOUND INTO

RAM, DIRECT TO HARD DISK, DIGITAL AUDIO OR VIDEO TAPE.

SCRATCHING A TURNTABLIST TECHNIQUE FOR RHYTHMI-CALLY MANIPULATING THE RECORD IN CONJUNCTION WITH THE CROSSFADER ON THE MIXER TO CHOP UP THE RHYTHM.

SELECTOR/SELECTA DJ.

SEQUENCER DEVICE THAT CAN MEMORISE AND SUBSEQUENTLY PLAY BACK A PRE-DETERMINED STRING OF PITCH, CONTROLLER AND TIMING INFORMATION. THIS INFORMATION CAN BE SENT TO AN INSTRUMENT, NOWADAYS USUALLY OVER **MIDI**, WHICH WILL THEN BE PLAYED AUTOMATICALLY.

SLIPMAT A BIT OF FELT YOU SLIP IN BETWEEN THE PLATTER AND THE RECORD TO HELP CONTROL THE VINYL.

SPINBACK A TECHNIQUE WHERE YOU SPIN THE RECORD BACK QUICKLY WITH ONE HAND AS YOU COME OUT OF A BEAT MIX.

STAB A SCRATCH TECHNIQUE WHICH IS MUCH THE SAME AS A CUT, EXCEPT THAT YOU PUSH THE RECORD FASTER AS YOU DROP IT INTO THE MIX, PRODUCING A HIGH-PITCHED SCRATCH SOUND.

STYLUS THE NEEDLE. THE TINY DIAMOND-TIPPED METAL ARM THAT READS THE GROOVE OF THE RECORD.

TECHNO A QUICKER, HARDER, AND SYNTHESISER-DRIVEN SOUND ORIGINATING IN DETROIT IN THE LATE EIGHTIES, WHICH COMBINED HOUSE WITH THE ELECTRONIC INFLU-ENCES FROM EUROPEAN PRODUCERS SUCH AS KRAFTWERK. THE SOUND PEAKED IN POPULARITY IN THE MID-NINETIES AND HAS PROGRESSIVELY BECOME MORE MINIMAL AND UNDERGROUND.

TOASTING WEST INDIAN RAGGA-STYLE RAPPING, OR 'CHATTING.'

TONE-ARM THE ARM THAT HOLDS THE CARTRIDGE , THAT HOLDS THE STYLUS THAT READS THE GROOVE OF THE RECORD.

TONE-ARM WEIGHT THE WEIGHT ON THE END OF THE TONE-ARM THAT ALLOWS YOU TO ADJUST THE AMOUNT OF 'TORQUE' ON THE NEEDLE.

TRANSFORMER SCRATCH CHOPPING UP THE MUTILAT-ED SCRATCH SOUNDS YOU ARE MAKING WITH ONE HAND ON THE RECORD, BY RHYTHMICALLY WAGGLING THE LINE-IN/PHONO SWITCH.

TURNTABLE THE DECKS. OR MORE SIMPLY THE SPINNING THING THAT PLAYS VINYL RECORDS.

WHITE LABEL A PROMOTIONAL COPY OF A VINYL RECORD WITH A BLANK, WHITE CENTRE STICKER, USUALLY WITH HANDWRITTEN INFORMATION ON IT.

WORKSTATION A SELF-CONTAINED MUSIC PRODUCTION CONSOLE COMPRISED OF A KEYBOARD, VARIOUS SYNTHESISER SOUNDS AND CONTROLLERS, AND A BUILT-IN DIGITAL RECORDER.

INDEX

Note: page numbers in **bold** refer to illustrations.